Her children rise up and call her blessed.

—

Proverbs 31:28 NKJV

The Busy Mom's Book of Inspiration

Published by Worthy Inspired, a division of Worthy Media, Inc.,
134 Franklin Road, Suite 200, Brentwood, Tennessee 37027.

Scripture references marked KJV are from the Holy Bible, King James Version

Scripture references marked NKJV are from the Holy Bible, New King James Version. Copyright © 1982 by Thomas Nelson, Inc. Used by permission.

Scripture references marked NCV are from the New Century Version®. Copyright © 1987, 1988, 1991 by Word Publishing, a division of Thomas Nelson, Inc. All rights reserved. Used by permission.

Scripture references marked HCSB are from the Holman Christian Standard Bible™ Copyright © 1999, 2000, 2001 by Holman Bible Publishers. Used by permission.

Scripture references marked NIV are from the Holy Bible, New International Version®, NIV® Copyright © 1973, 1978, 1984, 2011 by Biblica, Inc.® Used by permission. All rights reserved worldwide.

Scripture references marked NLT are from the Holy Bible. New Living Translation. Copyright © 1996 Tyndale Charitable Trust. Used by permission of Tyndale House Publishers.

Scripture references marked MSG are from the Message. Copyright © 1993, 1994, 1995, 1996, 2000, 2001, 2002. Used by permission of NavPress Publishing Group.

Cover Design by Kim Russell / Wahoo Designs
Page Layout by Bart Dawson

Printed in the United States of America

1 2 3 4 5—LBM—18 17 16 15 14

The Busy Mom's Book of Inspiration

Devotions to Renew Your Spirit

WORTHY
Inspired

A Message
to Busy Moms

Because you're reading this book, you probably answer to the name "Mom," "Mother," "Mommy," or some variation thereof—if so, congratulations. As a loving mother, you have been blessed by your children and by God.

Perhaps you received this book as a gift from a caring friend or husband. Or, perhaps, amid the hustle and bustle of your day, you managed to pick up this little book of your own accord. Either way, you will be blessed if you take the promises on these pages to heart.

This collection of quick and easy-to-read devotions is designed to provide hope and reminders of God's care for you. You matter to Him!

Motherhood is both a priceless gift from God and an unrelenting responsibility. Finding a few "extra" moments to spend reading another book may seem nearly impossible at this season of your life. Don't worry . . . there are no rules to follow here. This book is intended to remind you that, when it comes to the tough job of being a responsible mother, you and God, working together, are destined to do great things for your kids and for the world.

Chapter 1

A Mother's Love

Her children rise up and call her blessed.

Proverbs 31:28 NKJV

Few things in life are as precious or as enduring as a mother's love. From the time you held your firstborn in your arms, you knew somehow you had been given a supernatural ability to unconditionally love. It just happened. That capacity to love isn't depleted with the birth of another child either. It is multiplied.

Christ showed His love for us on the cross, and, as Christians, we are called upon to return Christ's love by sharing it. Sometimes love is easy (think cuddly puppies and sleeping children), and sometimes love is hard (think betrayed trust and rebellious teenagers). But God's Word is clear: We are to love our families and our neighbors without reservation or condition.

As a caring mother, you are not only shaping the lives of your loved ones, you are also, in a very real sense, reshaping eternity. It's a big job—a job so big, in fact, that God saw fit to entrust it to one of the most important people in His kingdom: a loving mom like you.

Love is something like the clouds that were
in the sky before the sun came out.
You cannot touch the clouds, you know;
but you feel the rain and know how glad
the flowers and the thirsty earth are to have it
after a hot day. You cannot touch love either;
but you feel the sweetness that it
pours into everything.

—

Annie Sullivan

Tips for Busy Moms

Be imaginative. There are so many ways to say, "I love you." Find them. Put love notes in lunch pails and on pillows; hug relentlessly; laugh, play, and pray with abandon. Remember that love is highly contagious, and that your task, as a parent, is to ensure that your children catch it.

— — — — — — — — — —

Be glad when they succeed and concerned when they struggle, but your personal happiness shouldn't rise and fall based upon what's going on with your child. That's too much pressure for anyone, especially a kid. Love them and care for them, but don't make them the center of the universe,[1]

iMOM.com

The Busy Mom's Book of Inspiration

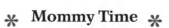

✳ Mommy Time ✳

What are some things you do for your kids to show them how much you love them?

_____

_____

_____

_____

_____

_____

_____

_____

_____

_____

_____

_____

_____

_____

_____

_____

First Things First

You shall have no other gods before Me.

Exodus 20:3 NKJV

There's not enough time in the day to do everything. You need to prioritize what absolutely has to be done and let go of unrealistic to-do lists that will only make you feel defeated at the end of the day. And your first priority is—and always should be—giving thanks to your Creator.

Whether you are a morning person or a night owl, giving thanks can be as natural as whispering, "Thank You, Jesus, for my child. Please give me the strength I need to do what You have planned for me."

As you think about the nature of your relationship with God, remember this: you will always have some type of relationship with Him. It is inevitable that your life must be lived in relationship to God. The question is not if you will have a relationship with Him; the burning question is if that relationship will be one that seeks to honor Him . . . or not.

Are you willing to place God first in your life? In your day? Thankfully, God is always available, He's always ready to listen and forgive, and He's waiting to hear from you now. Just tell Him what's on your heart. God knows already; He just likes to hear it from you.

Our ultimate aim in life is not to be
healthy, wealthy, prosperous, or problem free.
Our ultimate aim in life is to bring glory to God.

—

Anne Graham Lotz

Tips for Busy Moms

Any relationship that doesn't honor God is a relationship that is destined for problems, and soon (Hebrews 12:2). So strengthen your relationship with the Creator and ask Him for guidance as you build stronger ties with you souse and your children.

— — — — — — — — —

The key to organization is knowing what's a priority and what can wait. Experts suggest that you divide your to-do list into three sections: those things that need to be taken care of immediately, those that can get done anytime during the week, and those that are long-term or ongoing projects.[2]

Parents.com

The Busy Mom's Book of Inspiration

✳ **Mommy Time** ✳

What are some things you can do
with your kids to say "Thanks" to God?

_____

_____

_____

_____

_____

_____

_____

_____

_____

_____

_____

_____

_____

_____

_____

_____

_____

_____

Chapter 3

Too Busy?

Come to Me, all you who are weary and burdened,
and I will give you rest. Take My yoke upon you and learn
from Me, because I am gentle and humble in heart,
and you will find rest for your souls.
For My yoke is easy and My burden is light.
Matthew 11:28–30 HCSB

Endless tasks and responsibilities . . . that's what busy moms encounter every day. You may even be thinking right now of the next thing on your list, wondering if you will be able to check it off. Motherhood is so demanding that sometimes you may feel as if you have no time for yourself . . . and no time for God.

Has the busy pace of life robbed you of peace? If so, you are simply too busy for your own good. Through His Son Jesus, God offers you a peace that passes all human understanding, but He won't force His peace upon you. In order to experience it, you must slow down long enough to sense His presence and His love.

Today, as a gift to yourself and to your family, find a comfortable spot in your home and enjoy a cup of coffee or hot tea (and don't start clearing the coffee table!). Take a break long enough to claim the inner peace that is your spiritual birthright: the peace of Jesus Christ. It is offered freely; it has been paid for in full; it is yours for the asking. So ask. And then share.

In our tense, uptight society where folks are
rushing to make appointments they have already
missed, a good laugh can be a refreshing as
a cup of cold water in the desert.

—

Barbara Johnson

A Tip for Busy Moms

I'm enjoying the ride. Every day, I'm taking a few minutes to remind myself that these years won't last forever and that I should savor every single second with my kids. This self-talk seems to be working. Last week, I ditched all my Saturday errands and took my son to the movies. That night, I got into a tickle fight with my daughter that was so intense we both burped up pot roast. And I listened as they schemed about what Thanksgiving will be like when I'm old and they're in charge of the menu: There will be burgers and fries.[3]

Parents.com

The Busy Mom's Book of Inspiration

✳ **Mommy Time** ✳

How can you arrange your daily routine
to spend more time with God?

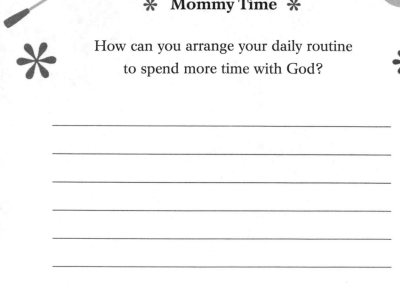

Chapter 4

Very Big Plans

No eye has seen, no ear has heard,
and no mind has imagined what God has
prepared for those who love him.

1 Corinthians 2:9 NLT

Sometimes it is difficult to look ahead into the future when you can only wrap your mind around this day—wearily falling into bed at night, only to start the whole thing over again tomorrow. The Bible makes it clear: God has plans—very big plans—for you and your family. That should give you hope. What you can't possibly see, He can.

As Christians, you and your family members should ask yourselves this question: "How closely can we make our plans match God's plans?" Do you have questions or concerns about the future? Take them to God in prayer. Do you have hopes and expectations? Talk to God about your dreams. Are you and your loved ones carefully planning for the days and weeks ahead? Consult God as you establish your priorities. Turn every concern over to your heavenly Father, and sincerely seek His guidance—prayerfully, earnestly, and often. Then, listen for His answers . . . and trust the answers that He gives.

The God who created and numbers the stars in
the heavens also numbers the hairs of my head.
He pays attention to very big things and
to very small ones. What matters to me
matters to Him, and that changes my life.

—

Elisabeth Elliot

Tips for Busy Moms

Sometimes, waiting faithfully for God's plan to unfold is more important than understanding God's plan. Ruth Bell Graham once said, "When I am dealing with an all-powerful, all-knowing God, I, as a mere mortal, must offer my petitions not only with persistence, but also with patience. Someday I'll know why." So even when you can't understand God's plans, you must trust Him and never lose faith!

— — — — — — — — —

Since you can't do everything, set your limits ahead of time. It's easier to say no if you already have a policy in place for yourself.[4]

GoodHousekeeping.com

✳ **Mommy Time** ✳

Do you have big plans for your kids?
What are some ways to make God
the center of those plans?

_____

_____

_____

_____

_____

_____

_____

_____

_____

_____

_____

_____

_____

_____

Chapter 5

The Power of Patience

Be joyful because you have hope.
Be patient when trouble comes, and pray at all times.

Romans 12:12 NCV

The rigors of motherhood can test the patience of the most even-tempered moms: From time to time, even the most well-behaved children may do things that worry us, or annoy us, or infuriate us. Why? Because they are children, and because they are human.

As loving parents, we must be patient with our children's shortcomings (just as they, too, must be patient with our own). But our patience must not be restricted to those who live under our care. We must also strive, to the best of our abilities, to exercise patience in all our dealings—from the way we treat our husbands to the way we treat the server at a restaurant—because our children are watching and learning.

Sometimes, patience is simply the price we pay for being responsible parents, and that's exactly as it should be. After all, think how patient our heavenly Father has been with us.

When we read of the great biblical leaders,
we see that it was not uncommon for God to ask
them to wait, not just a day or two, but for years,
until God was ready for them to act.

—

Gloria Gaither

A Tip for Busy Moms

Be patient with your child's impatience. Children are supposed to be more impulsive than adults; after all, they're still kids. So be understanding of your child's limitations and understanding of his or her imperfections.

The patience you show with your children now will one day be the patience they share with others. The kindness you plant in their tiny lives will grow into self-respect and respect for others. The love you naturally share with them will, in turn, be the love they have to give in the future.[5]

Mops.org/blog

✳ **Mommy Time** ✳

Do your kids do things that drive you
a little crazy? What are some specific things
you can do to become a more patient mom?

_____

_____

_____

_____

_____

_____

_____

_____

_____

_____

_____

_____

_____

_____

Chapter 6

He Renews

I will give you a new heart and
put a new spirit in you. . . .
Ezekiel 36:26 NIV

God intends that His children lead joyous lives filled with abundance and peace. But what does that look like in your home or work? Peace isn't that warm feeling when all is running smoothly—that's just an unusually good day. Peace is the assurance that, no matter the circumstances, God is still in control of your day.

Have you "tapped in" to the power of God, or are you muddling along under your own power? If you are weary, worried, fretful or fearful, then it is time to turn to a strength much greater than your own.

The Bible tells us that we can do all things through the power of our risen Savior, Jesus Christ. Our challenge, then, is clear: we must place Christ where He belongs: at the very center of our lives.

Are you tired or troubled? Turn your heart toward God in prayer. Are you weak or worried? Make the time to delve deeply into God's Holy Word. When you do, you'll discover that the Creator of the universe stands ready and able to create a new sense of wonderment and joy in you.

How motivating it has been for me to view my early morning devotions as time of retreat alone with Jesus, Who desires that I "come with Him by myself to a quiet place" in order to pray, read His Word, listen for His voice, and be renewed in my spirit.

—

Anne Graham Lotz

Tips for Busy Moms

Do you need time for yourself? Take it. Ruth Bell Graham observed, "It is important that we take time out for ourselves—for relaxation, for refreshment." Enough said.

— — — — — — — — —

Too busy and too stressed? Be choosey about your children's activities. Consider limiting children's activities to only one or two per kid per school year. Imagine how relaxing life could be with only one practice schedule, one weekend game, and one victory party.[6]

GoodHousekeeping.com

The Busy Mom's Book of Inspiration

✽ Mommy Time ✽

Find an extra moment in your day
to relax with God's Word.
What inspiration did you discover?

_____

_____

_____

_____

_____

_____

_____

_____

_____

_____

_____

_____

_____

Chapter 7

A Joyful Spirit

These things I have spoken to you, that My joy
may remain in you, and that your joy may be full.

John 15:11 NKJV

Are you a mom whose smile is evident for all to see? If so, congratulations: your joyful spirit serves as a powerful example to your family and friends. Whether you realize it or not, something as simple as a smiling face can have a positive impact on your family and the world.

Sometimes, amid the busyness of life here on earth, you may forfeit the joy that God intends for you to experience and to share. But even on life's most difficult days, you may rest assured that God is in His heaven, and He still cares for you. Peace and joy are God's precious gifts—gifts offered to you and your family daily.

And if you look in the mirror and realize your countenance does not reflect God's joy in your life—or any joy, for that matter—it's never too late to make a change. Start today. You have been blessed!

To a world that was spiritually dry and
populated with parched lives scorched by sin,
Jesus was the Living Water who would quench
the thirsty soul, saving it from "bondage"
and filling it with satisfaction and joy
and purpose and meaning.

—

Anne Graham Lotz

Tips for Busy Moms

Joy is contagious. Be sure to spread it around generously. Remember that a joyful family starts with joyful parents.

— — — — — — — — —

If negative and critical thinking have you in their grip, it's time to train yourself to redirect your thinking. If you don't, your negativity will affect your relationships with your husband and children. So the next time you have a critical thought, think about your child's smile or imagine your sweet children as babies. Imagine the rightness of God and how there is perfection in the love he has for us.[7]

iMOM.com

The Busy Mom's Book of Inspiration

✳ Mommy Time ✳

What are some specific ways that you
and your kids can share God's joy with
your neighbors and with the world?

_____

_____

_____

_____

_____

_____

_____

_____

_____

_____

_____

_____

_____

_____

_____

Chapter 8

The Right Kind of Example

Be an example to the believers in word, in conduct,
in love, in spirit, in faith, in purity.

1 Timothy 4:12 NKJV

Our children learn from the lessons we teach and the lives we live, but not necessarily in that order. The "record button" in our kids is constantly turned on. They see and hear things—good and bad—that help shape what they will one day do and say. Hopefully, what you are teaching your children to do lines up with your own behavior, in the home and especially in the community. No ones wants to hear, "Do as I say, not as I do."

What kind of example are you? Are you the kind of mother whose life serves as a genuine model of patience and righteousness? Are you the kind of mom whose actions, day

...n and day out, are based upon kindness, faithfulness, and a sincere love for the Lord? If so, you are not only blessed by God, but you are also a powerful force for good in a world that desperately needs positive influences such as yours.

Corrie ten Boom advised, "Don't worry about what you do not understand. Worry about what you do understand in the Bible but do not live by." And that's sound advice because our children and friends are watching . . . and so, for that matter, is God.

Heredity does not equip a child with proper attitudes; children learn what they are taught. We cannot expect proper behavior to appear magically.

—

James Dobson

Tips for Busy Moms

Your children will learn about life from many sources; the most important source can and should be you. But remember that the lectures you give are never as important as the ones you live.

— — — — — — — — —

With a heart full of gratitude, silently recount all of the things that you love about your life. Or, if you wish, jot them down so you can review your list at another time. You might start your list off by completing this unfinished sentence: "I really love _____."[8]

Live.FamilyEducation.com

✳ Mommy Time ✳

In what ways do your kids follow your example? And, how might you become a better example?

_____

_____

_____

_____

_____

_____

_____

_____

_____

_____

_____

_____

_____

_____

A Rule That's Golden

*So in everything, do to others what you would
have them do to you, for this sums up
the Law and the Prophets.*

Matthew 7:12 NIV

Is the Golden Rule one of the rules that governs your household? Hopefully so. Obeying it is a sure way to improve all your relationships—especially your relationships with the people who happen to live in your home. But the reverse is also true: if you or your loved ones ignore the Golden Rule, you're headed for trouble, and fast.

God's Word makes it clear: we are to treat others with respect, kindness, fairness, and courtesy. If you have more than one child, teach them to treat their siblings the way they would want to be treated. Sometimes it's not easy, but it can be done! And God knows we can do so if we try with His help—which He stands ready to give.

So, Mom, as you fulfill your many obligations, be sure to weave the thread of kindness into the fabric of your day. When you do, everybody wins . . . especially you.

I put a lot of emphasis on how to treat people.
The reason for this is simple. The real success of
our personal lives and careers can best be measured
by the relationships we have with the people most
dear to us—our family, friends, and coworkers.
If we fail in this aspect of our lives, no matter how
vast our worldly possessions or how
high on the corporate ladder we climb,
we will have achieved very little.

—

Mary Kay Ash

Tips for Busy Moms

When you live according to the principle of the Golden Rule, your children will notice, and the results will be as good as gold . . . make that better than gold!

— — — — — — — — —

Teaching virtues is first and foremost the job of parents. Virtues are more effectively caught than taught. Children are most likely to develop the virtues their parents model. Children best learn from their parents that virtues are both valuable and essential, which motivates them to make the effort to learn and practice them.[9]

iMOM.com

✳ **Mommy Time** ✳

Think of a few occasions when your kids
demonstrated virtues like respect, kindness,
fairness, or courtesy. Jot them down and
then congratulate your children.

_____

_____

_____

_____

_____

_____

_____

_____

_____

_____

_____

_____

_____

_____

Chapter 10

Maintaining Proper Perspective

*Your attitude should be the same
that Christ Jesus had.*

Philippians 2:5 NLT

Even if you're the world's most thoughtful mom, you may, from time to time, lose perspective—it happens on those days when life seems out of whack and the pressures of motherhood seem overwhelming. What's needed is a fresh perspective, a restored sense of balance . . . and God.

If a temporary loss of perspective has left you worried, exhausted, or both, it's time to readjust your thought patterns. Negative thoughts are habit-forming; thankfully, so are positive ones. With practice, you can form the habit of focusing on God's priorities and your possibilities. When you

you'll spend less time fretting about your challenges and more time praising God for His gifts.

So today, right this minute, pray for a sense of balance and perspective. And remember: your thoughts are intensely powerful things, so handle them with care.

Earthly fears are no fears at all.
Answer the big questions of eternity,
and the little questions of life
fall into perspective.

—

Max Lucado

A Tip for Busy Moms

It's important to remember that only God is perfect. I'm not. You're not. Your spouse isn't. Your boss/coworkers aren't. Your neighbors, church, kids, pastors, friends . . . all not perfect. Only God is perfect.

What I am saying is that today is the "perfect" time for you and I to take our bosses, spouses, neighbors, kids, pastors, friends and perhaps OURSELVES off the perfect pedestal because in the space between Perfect and me you'll find your "Good enough!"[10]

247moms.com

✳ **Mommy Time** ✳

What are some things in your life
you feel negatively about?

_____

_____

_____

_____

_____

_____

_____

_____

_____

_____

_____

_____

_____

Now, spend a few moments thinking about
how God would respond to your list.

Chapter 11

Family Prayer and Worship

But as for me and my household, we will serve the Lord.

Joshua 24:15 NIV

When you encourage your family to worship God, you are to be praised. But worship is more than just going to church on Sundays and singing praise songs and hymns. Worship is a verb—it requires action on our part, at church and at home. From beautiful music to the wonder of nature to words of praise—all can be enjoyed as a family.

Do you and your family pray only at mealtimes, or do you also extend "breath" prayers throughout the day and prayers of gratitude at bedtime? Ours is a society in which too many parents have abandoned, maybe unintentionally, the moral leadership of their families, often with tragic consequences.

Every day provides opportunities to put God where He belongs: at the center of our hearts. May we worship Him and only Him. So, as you go about your daily activities, remember God's instructions: "Rejoice always, pray continually, give thanks in all circumstances; for this is God's will for you in Christ Jesus" (1 Thessalonians 5:16–18 NIV). God is always listening, and He always wants to hear from you and your family.

There is, however, equally great incentive to worship and love God in the thought that, for some unfathomable reason, He wants me as His friend, and desires to be my friend, and has given His Son to die for me in order to realize this purpose. Not merely that we know God, but that He knows us.

—

J. I. Packer

Tips for Busy Moms

Don't ever be embarrassed to pray: Are you embarrassed to bow your head in a restaurant? Don't be; it's the people who aren't praying who should be embarrassed!

— — — — — — — — —

Ask for help! You don't have to be Supermom and do everything yourself. Recruit other resources when you're running short on time (and sanity). Consider bartering with another mom; she can run some errands for you one day and you can watch her son for two hours another day.[11]

Parents.com

The Busy Mom's Book of Inspiration

✳ **Mommy Time** ✳

Spend a few moments writing prayers
for your kids and your family.

_____

_____

_____

_____

_____

_____

_____

_____

_____

_____

_____

_____

_____

_____

_____

Chapter 12

Making Time
to Praise God

*So through Jesus let us always offer to God our sacrifice
of praise, coming from lips that speak his name.*

Hebrews 13:15 NCV

Sometimes we take for granted the treasures that God
has given us. Our children, family, home, jobs, friends.
talents—sure, we are thankful for them, but at times they can
feel "expected," as if they will always be there.

God sent His only Son to die for you; He gave you a
family to care for and to love; He's given you yet another day
of life, filled to the brim with opportunities to celebrate and
to serve. What should you do in return for God's priceless
gifts? Praise Him!

As you gaze upon a passing cloud, or marvel at a glorious sunset, think of what God has done for you. Every time

you notice a gift from the Giver of all things good, praise Him. His works are marvelous, His gifts are beyond understanding, and His love endures forever.

I am to praise God for all things,
regardless of where they seem to originate.
Doing this is the key to receiving
the blessings of God.
Praise will wash away my resentments.

—

Catherine Marshall

Tips for Busy Moms

Remember that it always pays to praise your Creator. That's why thoughtful moms (like you) make it a habit to carve out quiet moments throughout the day to praise God.

— — — — — — — — —

The cliché "There's so much to do and so little time" was surely coined by a working mother. One way to help prioritize household and home-management tasks is to make a daily to-do list (a simple yellow legal pad is my favorite to-do list tool). Spending five minutes a day making this list will help you save time over the long haul.[12]

FocusontheFamily.com

✳ **Mommy Time** ✳

Take a few moments to make a list of special
people in your life and the blessings
God has given you through them.

_____

_____

_____

_____

_____

_____

_____

_____

_____

_____

_____

_____

_____

Now, thank Him for those blessings.

Chapter 13

Every Day with God

Morning by morning he wakens me and opens
my understanding to his will. The Sovereign Lord
has spoken to me, and I have listened.

Isaiah 50:4–5 NLT

There's something special about a new morning. Whatever happened yesterday is past, and today is a clean slate. Each new day is a gift from God, and wise moms spend a few quiet moments each morning thanking the Giver. Daily life is woven together with the threads of habit, and no habit is more important to our spiritual health than the discipline of daily prayer and devotion to the Creator.

When we begin each day with heads bowed and hearts lifted, we remind ourselves that God is with us—nothing will happen to us that surprises Him or exceeds His sovereignty. And if we are wise, we align our priorities for the coming day with the teachings and commandments that God has given us through His Holy Word.

Are you seeking to change some aspect of your life? Then take time out of your hectic schedule to sit with your heavenly Father. Do you seek to improve your study of God's Word? If so, ask for God's wisdom as you focus on a passage of Scripture. But don't expect to open your Bible today and be wise tomorrow. Wisdom is not like a mushroom; it does not spring up overnight. It is, instead, like an oak tree that starts as a tiny acorn, grows into a sapling, and eventually reaches up to the sky, tall and strong. And it all starts with a few quiet moments right now . . .

Our devotion to God is strengthened when we offer Him a fresh commitment each day.

—

Elizabeth George

Tips for Busy Moms

How much time can you spare? Decide how much of your time God deserves, and then give it to Him. Don't organize your day so that God gets "what's left." Give Him what you honestly believe He deserves.

— — — — — — — — —

Put those kids to work! While kids need down-time and playtime, some assigned household chores are also good for them—and great for you. Chores instill independence and responsibility in children, and help busy parents save time.[13]

Live.FamilyEducation.com

The Busy Mom's Book of Inspiration

✳ Mommy Time ✳

What are some things you can have
your kids do to help you gain an extra
few minutes in your day to spend with God?

_____

_____

_____

_____

_____

_____

_____

_____

_____

_____

_____

_____

_____

_____

Chapter 14

Big Dreams

"No eye has seen, no ear has heard,
and no mind has imagined what God
has prepared for those who love him."

1 Corinthians 2:9 NLT

Are you a mom who believes that God has big plans in store for you and your family? Hopefully so. Yet sometimes, especially if you've recently experienced a life-altering disappointment, you may find it difficult to envision a brighter future for yourself and your loved ones. If so, it's time to reconsider your own capabilities . . . and God's.

Your heavenly Father created you with unique gifts and untapped talents—your job is to tap them. Ask yourself: "What am I passionate about?" Maybe it's photography or cooking, writing a blog or teaching yoga. If you're not sure what your gifts are, ask a close friend what she thinks you might be good at. When you do, you'll begin to feel an increasing sense of confidence in yourself and in your future.

It takes courage to dream big dreams. You will discover that courage when you do three things: accept the past, trust God to handle the future, and make the most of the time He has given you today.

Nothing is too difficult for God, and no dreams are too big for Him—not even yours. So start living—and dreaming—accordingly.

I look back now and realize that the gift of
a true friend is that she sees you not the way you
see yourself or the way others see you.
A true friend sees you for who you are
and who you can become.

—

Robin Jones Gunn

A Tip for Busy Moms

You can dream big dreams, but you can never out-dream God. His plans for you and your loved ones are even bigger than you can imagine.

— — — — — — — — —

Today, I challenge you to take 10 minutes and sit quietly and ask God the big question "What are you asking me/us to do?"—"Why shouldn't we do it?"

Stop using those 100 reasons as to why life is getting in the way; let's instead surrender our agenda for His and see what life is like when we just do it, because there is no reason we shouldn't and watch your life change by how he wants to use you.[14]

247moms.com

The Busy Mom's Book of Inspiration

✳ **Mommy Time** ✳

What are some of your big dreams?
And, what dreams do you have for your children? ✳

_____

_____

_____

_____

_____

_____

_____

_____

_____

_____

_____

_____

_____

_____

_____

_____

_____

Chapter 15

God Can Handle It

For I am the Lord your God who takes hold
of your right hand and says to you,
Do not fear; I will help you.

Isaiah 41:13 NIV

It's a promise that is made over and over again in the Bible: Whatever "it" is, God can handle it. No problems are too big for Him.

Life isn't easy; life isn't fair. Far from it! Your family may experience a job loss or a health crisis. You may have worries about the future or care for a child with special needs. But even then, even during your darkest moments, you're protected by a loving heavenly Father—sheltered in the shadow of His wings.

When you're worried, God can reassure you with His promises; when you're sad, God can comfort you with His

Spirit. When your heart is broken, God is not just near; He is here. So release all that you are trying to carry by yourself. Let your heavenly Father hold your hand as you trust Him with all your cares.

What is needed for happy effectual service is simply to put your work into the Lord's hand, and leave it there. Do not take it to Him in prayer, saying, "Lord, guide me, Lord, give me wisdom, Lord, arrange for me," and then arise from your knees, and take the burden all back, and try to guide and arrange for yourself. Leave it with the Lord, and remember that what you trust to Him you must not worry over nor feel anxious about. Trust and worry cannot go together.

Hannah Whitall Smith

Tips for Busy Moms

God is in control of His world and your world. Rely upon Him. Vance Havner writes, "When we get to a place where it can't be done unless God does it, God will do it!" So teach your children that God can handle anything.

— — — — — — — — —

Stress and motherhood go hand in hand. We pretty much hit the ground running and don't stop until our heads hit the pillow. But, if we don't deal with our stress and anger levels, our relationship with our children will reflect that tension.[15]

iMOM.com

✳ **Mommy Time** ✳

What are some things in your life you need
to hand over to God?

_____

_____

_____

_____

_____

_____

_____

_____

_____

_____

_____

_____

_____

_____

Chapter 16

Those Difficult Days

We are pressed on every side by troubles, but not crushed.
We are perplexed, but not driven to despair.

2 Corinthians 4:8 NLT

As every mother knows, some days are just plain difficult—days when the baby is sick, the laundry is piled high, and the bills are piled even higher. When we find ourselves overtaken by the inevitable frustrations of life, we must catch ourselves, take a deep breath, and lift our thoughts upward. Although we are here on earth struggling to rise above the distractions of the day, we need never struggle alone. God is here—eternal and faithful—and, if we reach out to Him, He will restore perspective and peace to our souls.

Sometimes even the most devout Christian moms can become discouraged, and you are no exception. After all, you live in a broken world where expectations can be high and demands can be even higher.

If you find yourself enduring a difficult day, try to view as an opportunity for God to act. On some days, you'll give Him lots of opportunities! Trust Him; He is faithful to see you through to the end.

When the hard times of life come,
we know that no matter how tragic
the circumstances seem, no matter how long
the spiritual drought, no matter how long and
dark the days, the sun is sure to break through;
the dawn will come.

—

Gloria Gaither

Tips for Busy Moms

Every mom faces difficult days, but Christians face their challenges with God as their partner.

— — — — — — — — —

Establish a Routine: It's not always easy to make it out of the house on time when you have an established morning routine, but it's definitely more difficult if you're flying by the seat of your pants. Make sure that you establish a set routine for each morning that includes feeding every member of the family, making sure that everyone's dressed appropriately and that everyone is ready to troop down to the car or school bus when the time comes.[16]

247moms.com

The Busy Mom's Book of Inspiration

✳ **Mommy Time** ✳

✳ What are some of the distractions in your daily routine that you can change? ✳

_____

_____

_____

_____

_____

_____

_____

_____

_____

_____

_____

_____

_____

_____

_____

_____

_____

Chapter 17

Choose to Forgive

When you are praying, if you are angry with someone,
forgive him so that your Father in heaven
will also forgive your sins.

Mark 11:25 NCV

Even the most mild-mannered moms will, on occasion, have reason to become angry with the inevitable shortcomings of family members and friends. But wise women are quick to forgive others, just as God has forgiven them.

Forgiveness is God's commandment, but oh how difficult a commandment it can be to follow. We feel as if we have a right to hold a grudge when we've been wronged. Being frail, fallible, imperfect human beings, we are quick to anger, quick to blame, slow to forgive, and even slower to forget. No matter. Even when forgiveness is difficult, God's Word is clear.

If, in your heart, you hold bitterness against someone, forgive—even if that person isn't sorry. If there exists even one person, alive or dead, whom you have not forgiven, follow God's commandment and His will for your life: forgive. If you are embittered against yourself for some past mistake or shortcoming, forgive. It will bring freedom. Then, to the best of your abilities, forget, and move on. Bitterness and regret are not part of God's plan for your life. Forgiveness is.

Forgiveness is actually the best revenge
because it not only sets us free from the person
we forgive, but it frees us to move into
all that God has in store for us.

—

Stormie Omartian

Tips for Busy Moms

Face facts: forgiveness can be a very hard thing to do. No matter. God instructs us to forgive others (and to keep forgiving them), period. As a parent, you must explain to your child that forgiving another person—even when it's difficult—is the right thing to do.

— — — — — — — — —

But how in the world do we keep ourselves from grumbling, complaining, and being frustrated amid the demanding role of motherhood? When it comes to living an everyday mom life in the right way, our motto should be "attitude is everything." And when it comes to advice on attitude, Proverbs 15:13-15 is a great place to go.[17]

iMOM.com

The Busy Mom's Book of Inspiration

✳ **Mommy Time** ✳

Who do you need to forgive in your heart?
Do you need to seek forgiveness
for something you may have done?

_____

_____

_____

_____

_____

_____

_____

_____

_____

_____

_____

_____

_____

Chapter 18

The Gift of Eternal Life

*For God so loved the world that he gave his one
and only Son, that whoever believes in him
shall not perish but have eternal life.*

John 3:16 NIV

Your life here on earth is merely a preparation for a far different life to come: the eternal life that God promises to those who welcome His Son into their hearts.

When you're in the middle of "doing life," it's hard to look beyond your tasks and contemplate eternity. Sometimes it's hard to contemplate next Wednesday! God's vision is not burdened by such limitations: His plans extend throughout all eternity. Thus, God's plans for you are not limited to the ups and downs of everyday life. Your heavenly Father has bigger things in mind . . . much bigger things.

As you struggle with the inevitable hardships and disappointments of life, remember that God has invited you to accept His abundance not only for today but also for all eternity. So keep things in perspective. Although you will encounter occasional defeats in this world, you'll have all eternity to celebrate the ultimate victory in the next.

I can still hardly believe it. I, with shriveled,
bent fingers, atrophied muscles, gnarled knees,
and no feeling from the shoulders down,
will one day have a new body—light, bright and
clothed in righteousness—powerful and dazzling.

—

Joni Eareckson Tada

Tips for Busy Moms

God offers a priceless gift: the gift of eternal life. God has created heaven and given you a way to get there. Make sure you share the way with your children.

— — — — — — — — —

Be real. Being worthy of imitation doesn't mean putting on a perfect front and hiding the rest. We need to let our children see how we handle life's challenges— from the big ones, to the little ones. Even if we struggle while we do it, our kids need to see how we handle real life.[18]

iMOM.com

The Busy Mom's Book of Inspiration

✳ **Mommy Time** ✳

Take a moment to reflect on the gifts God
has waiting for us in Heaven
and the cost of our salvation.

_____

_____

_____

_____

_____

_____

_____

_____

_____

_____

_____

_____

_____

_____

Chapter 19

Fitness Matters

Whatever you eat or drink or whatever you do,
you must do all for the glory of God.

1 Corinthians 10:31 NLT

Physical fitness is a choice, a choice that requires discipline—it's as simple as that. Notice I didn't say, "It's as easy as that." Why? Because it's usually more fun to eat a second piece of cake than it is to jog a second lap around the track. Just as we are to lead disciplined lives with our spiritual habits, we need to take care of our bodies that God gave us. It's the only one we've got until we get to heaven.

We live in a world in which leisure is glorified and consumption is commercialized. But God has other plans. He did not create us for lives of gluttony or laziness; He created us for far greater things.

God has a plan for every aspect of your life, and His plan includes provisions for your physical health. But, He

...cts you to do your fair share of the work! Don't be over-
...elmed with the idea of yet another drain on your time—a
...tness routine. Making healthy food choices while still enjoying some of your favorite foods, coupled with brisk walks in
your neighborhood, are simple changes that can bring energy
to your day. It's a win-win-win—you have more energy for
your family, you feel better about yourself, and God is hon-
ored with your commitment to care for His gift . . . you!

People are funny. When they are young,
they will spend their health to get wealth.
Later, they will gladly pay all they have
trying to get their health back.

—

John Maxwell

Tips for Busy Moms

If you're trying to reshape your physique or your life, don't try to do it alone—get the kids involved, too. You can also ask for the support and encouragement of your husband or friends. You could even make play dates with one of your child's friends and their mom to exercise. You'll improve your odds of success if you enlist your own cheering section.

— — — — — — — — —

Don't skip breakfast! A cup of coffee does not equal a healthy start to the day (and no, two cups don't make it better). Studies have found that people feel more satisfied by food eaten in the morning, a feeling that can translate into better energy for your day.[19]

Webmd.com

The Busy Mom's Book of Inspiration

✻ Mommy Time ✻

What are some activities you can do with
your kids each day to exercise?

_____

_____

_____

_____

_____

_____

_____

_____

_____

_____

_____

_____

_____

_____

_____

Chapter 20

Your Noisy World

Quiet down before God, be prayerful before him.

Psalm 37:7 MSG

F ace it: We live in a noisy world, a world filled with distractions, frustrations, and complications. Your phone dings another text alert; the TV drones on in the background; the kids are fussing at each other. But if we allow those distractions to separate us from God's peace, we do ourselves a profound disservice.

Are you one of those busy moms who rush through the day with scarcely a single moment for quiet contemplation and prayer? If so, it's time to be intentional about peace and quiet. If your house is a little cluttered, at least have one spot (maybe your bedroom) that is a haven—a place where you can shut the door, silence the phone, light a scented candle, and be still for even a few minutes.

Nothing is more important than the time you spend ith your Savior. So be still and claim the inner peace that is there for the taking. If even Jesus required quiet moments away from the crowd to spend with His Father, shouldn't you?

Among the enemies to devotion,
none is so harmful as distractions.
Whatever excites the curiosity, scatters
the thoughts, disquiets the heart, absorbs
the interests, or shifts our life focus from
the kingdom of God within us to
the world around us—that is a distraction;
and the world is full of them.

—

A. W. Tozer

Tips for Busy Moms

The Right Way to Start the Day: Begin each day with a few minutes of quiet time to organize your thoughts. During this time, read at least one uplifting Bible passage and thus begin your day on a positive, productive note.

— — — — — — — — —

When you're feeling overloaded, try turning down the background noise in your life by "unplugging" some of these electronic taskmasters.[20]

Parenting.com

✳ **Mommy Time** ✳

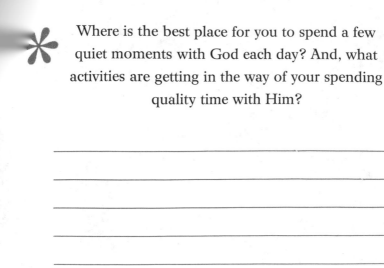

Where is the best place for you to spend a few
quiet moments with God each day? And, what
activities are getting in the way of your spending
quality time with Him?

_____

_____

_____

_____

_____

_____

_____

_____

_____

_____

_____

_____

_____

_____

Chapter 21

When Mistakes
Are Made

Therefore, if anyone is in Christ, he is a new creation;
the old has gone, the new has come!

2 Corinthians 5:17 NIV

As parents, we are far from perfect. So were our parents. And, without question, our children are imperfect as well. Thus, mistakes are bound to happen.

Has someone in your family or close to your family experienced a recent setback? If so, it's time to start looking for the lesson that God is trying to teach. It's time to learn what needs to be learned, change what needs to be changed, and move on.

One of the greatest lessons you can teach your children is to humble yourself and admit to them when you've made a mistake. They need to see you goof up sometimes just like

...ey do, and some "I'm sorry's" need to be said. They will be able to learn from their mistakes if they see a mommy who does the same.

If you have made a mistake, even serious mistakes,
there is always another chance for you,
for this thing we call "failure" is not
the falling down, but the staying down.

—

Mary Pickford

Tips for Busy Moms

No parent is perfect, not even you. Consequently, you will make mistakes from time to time (and yes, you might even lose your temper). When you are wrong admit it. When you do, your children will learn that it's far better to fix problems than to ignore them.

— — — — — — — — —

Your goal is not to create a perfect life devoid of bumps and interruptions; it is to smooth out what you can, create systems that help control the chaos and then learn to go with the flow when all else fails.[21]

FocusontheFamily.com

The Busy Mom's Book of Inspiration

✳ Mommy Time ✳

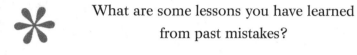

What are some lessons you have learned
from past mistakes?

_____

_____

_____

_____

_____

_____

_____

_____

_____

_____

_____

_____

_____

_____

_____

_____

Chapter 22

Trust the Shepherd

The Lord is my shepherd; I shall not want.

Psalm 23:1 NKJV

In the popular 23rd Psalm, David teaches us that God is like a watchful shepherd caring for His flock. No wonder these verses have provided comfort and hope for generations of believers.

When God looks at you, He sees someone who is precious and valuable. Just like you have watched your own sleeping baby, God hears every breath you take, so you need never be afraid. Sheep cannot care for themselves without a devoted shepherd; it is no coincidence the Bible compares God's children to needy sheep.

On occasion, you will confront circumstances that trouble you to the very core of your soul. When you are afraid, trust in God. When you are worried, turn your concerns

...er to Him. When you are anxious, be still and listen for the quiet assurance of God's promises. And then, place your life in His hands. He is your shepherd today and throughout eternity. Trust the Shepherd.

Christ reigns in his church as shepherd-king.
He has supremacy, but it is the superiority
of a wise and tender shepherd over his needy
and loving flock. He commands and receives
obedience, but it is willing obedience of
well-cared-for-sheep, offered joyfully to their
beloved Shepherd, whose voice they know
so well. He rules by the force of love
and the energy of goodness.

—

C. H. Spurgeon

Tips for Busy Moms

You know that "God is love." Now, it's your responsibility to make certain that your children know it, too.

— — — — — — — — —

One of the most important lessons that you can ever learn is to trust God for everything—not some things, not most things . . . in everything!

— — — — — — — — —

God sees your potential even when you and others around you don't. You only see where you are at right now but He sees where He can take you . . . if you let Him![22]

Busymomsconnect.com

✳ **Mommy Time** ✳

Think about times when God demonstrated
His faithfulness to you and your family.
What did you learn from those times?

_____

_____

_____

_____

_____

_____

_____

_____

_____

_____

_____

_____

_____

_____

Chapter 23

To Shop or Not to Shop?

Don't hoard treasure down here where it gets eaten by moths and corroded by rust or—-worse!—stolen by burglars. Stockpile treasure in heaven, where it's safe from moth and rust and burglars. It's obvious, isn't it? The place where your treasure is, is the place you will most want to be, and end up being.

Matthew 6:19–21 MSG

In the demanding world in which we live, financial prosperity can be a good thing, but spiritual prosperity is profoundly more important. Yet our society leads us to believe otherwise. The world glorifies material possessions, personal fame, and physical beauty. These things, of course, are totally unimportant to God. God sees the human heart, and that's what matters to Him.

Does this mean we can't enjoy our possessions? No, we can certainly be blessed by our home and things, and bless others too. But if the accumulation of things is what we are striving for, then our treasure is in the wrong place.

As you establish spending priorities for yourself and your family, remember this: The world will do everything it can to convince you that "stuff" is important. The world will tempt you to value fortune above faith and possessions above peace. Be thankful for what you have, and trust God for what you need.

It's sobering to contemplate how much time,
effort, sacrifice, compromise, and attention
we give to acquiring and increasing
our supply of something that is
totally insignificant in eternity.

—

Anne Graham Lotz

Tips for Busy Moms

Material possessions may seem appealing at first, but they pale in comparison to the spiritual gifts that God gives to those who put Him first. Count yourself among that number.

— — — — — — — — —

Too Much Stuff: Too much stuff doesn't ensure happiness. In fact, having too much stuff can actually prevent happiness.

— — — — — — — — —

Owning things isn't bad, but we have to be honest about the fact that the more we own, the more we're required to maintain. At some point, the cost of ownership is too much, and you'd be happier with less stuff.[23]

iMOM.com

✳ **Mommy Time** ✳

What are some ways to show your kids
the spending habits that reflect the values
that you want them to imitate?

_____

_____

_____

_____

_____

_____

_____

_____

_____

_____

_____

_____

_____

_____

_____

Chapter 24

Time: A Treasure from God

So teach us to number our days,
that we may gain a heart of wisdom.

Psalm 90:12 NKJV

As every mother knows all too well, there simply isn't enough time to do everything we want—and need—to do. That's why we should be so very careful about the ways that we choose to spend the time that God has given us.

Time is a nonrenewable gift from the Creator. But sometimes, we treat our time here on earth as if it were not a gift at all: We may be tempted to invest our lives in petty diversions or in trivial pursuits. But our Father in heaven beckons each of us to a higher calling. This doesn't mean we can't ever relax, thus creating guilt over "vegging out" from time to time. Sometimes moms just need a break from an already-packed day. We just shouldn't waste opportunities that God gives us to produce good things from the twenty-four hours He gives us each day.

Each waking moment holds the potential to do a good deed, to say a kind word, or to offer a heartfelt prayer. Our challenge, as moms, is to use our time wisely in the service of God's work and in accordance with His plan for our lives.

Overcommitment and time pressures are
the greatest destroyers of marriages and families.
It takes time to develop any friendship,
whether with a loved one or with God himself.

—

James Dobson

Tips for Busy Moms

How much time should you dedicate to your family? The answer is straightforward: You should invest large quantities of high-quality time in caring for your clan. As you nurture your loved ones, you should do your very best to ensure that God remains squarely at the center of your family's life. When you do, He will bless you—and yours—in ways that you could have scarcely imagined.

— — — — — — — — —

You aren't going to be able to keep up with work or your family if you don't take care of yourself. "Me" time is very important for busy moms. Even if it's only 15 to 20 minutes a day, you need to make time for yourself.[24]

Sheknows.com

The Busy Mom's Book of Inspiration

✳ **Mommy Time** ✳

What are some fun new things you can do with your kids to spend some quality time?

_____

_____

_____

_____

_____

_____

_____

_____

_____

_____

_____

_____

_____

_____

_____

Chapter 25

Choosing to Be Kind

Be kind and compassionate to one another,
forgiving each other,
just as in Christ God forgave you.

Ephesians 4:32 NIV

Kindness is a choice. Sometimes, when we feel happy or generous, we find it easy to be kind. Other times, when we are discouraged or tired, we can scarcely summon the energy to utter a single kind word. But, God's commandment is clear: He intends that we make the conscious choice to treat others with kindness and respect, no matter our circumstances, no matter our emotions.

In the busyness of daily life, it is easy to lose focus and become frustrated. Our children see the "real" us rather than the cleaned-up version we often show others. We are imperfect human beings struggling to manage our lives as best we can, but we often fall short. When we are distracted or disappointed, we may neglect to share a kind word or deed. This oversight hurts others, but it hurts us most of all.

Today, slow yourself down and be alert for people who need your smile, your kind words, your helping hand—start with your family.

If we have the true love of God in our hearts,
we will show it in our lives. We will not
have to go up and down the earth proclaiming it.
We will show it in everything we say or do.

—

D. L. Moody

Tips for Busy Moms

Kindness Every Day: Kindness should be part of our lives every day, not just on the days when we feel good. Don't try to be kind some of the time, and don't try to be kind to some of the people you know. Instead, try to be kind all of the time, and try to be kind to all the people you know. Remember, the Golden Rule starts with you!

— — — — — — — — —

Today, as you talk to your child, replace sarcasm with kindness.[25]

iMOM.com

The Busy Mom's Book of Inspiration

✳ **Mommy Time** ✳

What are some random acts of kindness
you can do with your kids?

Chapter 26

Enthusiasm for the Journey

Don't befriend angry people or associate with
hot-tempered people, or you will learn to be like them.

Proverbs 22:24–25 NLT

Enthusiasm, like other human emotions, is contagious. If you associate with hope-filled, enthusiastic people, their enthusiasm will have a tendency to lift your spirits. But if you find yourself spending too much time in the company of "Debbie Downers," or cynics, your thoughts, like theirs, will tend to be negative.

So, Mom, as you consider ways to improve your spiritual and emotional health, ask yourself if you're associating with positive people. If so, then you can rest assured you're availing yourself of a priceless gift: the encouragement.

Today, look for reasons to celebrate God's countless blessings. And while you're at it, look for upbeat friends who will join with you in the celebration. You'll be better for their company, and you, in turn, will be a positive light for someone else—as well as your children.

Optimism is the faith that leads to achievement.
Nothing can be done without
hope and confidence.

—

Helen Keller

Tips for Busy Moms

Don't wait for enthusiasm to find you . . . go looking for it. Look at your life and your relationships as exciting adventures. Don't wait for life to spice itself; spice things up yourself.

— — — — — — — — —

Be enthusiastic about your faith. John Wesley wrote, "You don't have to advertise a fire. Get on fire for God and the world will come to watch you burn." When you allow yourself to become extremely enthusiastic about your faith, other people will notice—and so will God.

✳ Mommy Time ✳

Are there some negative things in your life
that you can change or do away with? And,
if you were able to eliminate these negatives,
how would it impact your family?

_____

_____

_____

_____

_____

_____

_____

_____

_____

_____

_____

_____

_____

_____

Chapter 27

The Power of Perseverance

You need to persevere so that when you have done
the will of God, you will receive what he has promised.

Hebrews 10:36 NIV

Someone once said, "Life is a marathon, not a sprint." The same can be said for motherhood. Motherhood requires courage, perseverance, determination, and, of course, an unending supply of motherly love.

Jesus, finished what He began. Despite the torture He endured, despite the shame of the cross, Jesus was steadfast in His faithfulness to God. We, too, must remain faithful, especially during times of hardship.

Are you tired? Do you feel as if you will never get a good night's sleep? Ask God for strength. Are you discouraged? Maybe you long for someone—anyone—just to say, "How was your day?" Be certain that God cares about your day. Are you frustrated? Do you tie yourself up in knots trying to solve everyone's problems? Pray that God will show you what you're responsible for and leave everything else with Him. With God's help, you will find the strength to be the kind of mother that makes her heavenly Father beam with pride.

In times of doubt or trouble, you must patiently persevere and trust in the capable hands of your Creator. Whatever your problem, He can handle it. Your job is to keep persevering until He does.

God knows our situation; He will not judge us
as if we had no difficulties to overcome.
What matters is the sincerity and perseverance
of our will to overcome them.

—

C. S. Lewis

Tips for Busy Moms

The next time you find your courage tested to the limit, remember that God is as near as your next breath, and remember that He offers strength and comfort to His children. He is your shield, your protector, and your deliverer. Call upon Him in your hour of need and then be comforted. Whatever your challenge, whatever your trouble, God can give you the strength to persevere, and that's exactly what you should ask Him to do.

— — — — — — — — —

Give everyone a job. Whether it's sorting laundry, licking stamps, or picking things up, there are chores that even the littlest of helpers can do.[26]

Parents.com

✳ Mommy Time ✳

Think of people you know who have
experienced hardship but refused to quit.
Jot down their names and talk to your kids
about the rewards of perseverance.

_____

_____

_____

_____

_____

_____

_____

_____

_____

_____

_____

_____

_____

_____

Chapter 28

Thanksgiving Now

In everything give thanks;
for this is the will of God in Christ Jesus for you.

1 Thessalonians 5:18 NKJV

As a busy mom who takes her responsibilities seriously, sometimes you may find yourself caught up in the demands of everyday life, and it's only natural that you might fail to pause and thank your Creator for His blessings. But if the pressures of motherhood have caused you to make a ongoing habit of ignoring God's gifts, it's time to rethink your habits, your obligations, and your priorities.

Whenever you slow down and express your sincere gratitude to the Father, you enrich your own life and the lives of your loved ones. You know that warm feeling you get when your child looks up at you and says, "Thank you, Mommy." Well, God feels the same way when He hears thankfulness from His children.

Let words of thanks be a part of your daily routine. Yes, God has blessed you beyond measure, and you owe Him everything, including your eternal praise every day . . . starting now.

Thanksgiving or complaining—these words express two contrastive attitudes of the souls of God's children in regard to His dealings with them. The soul that gives thanks can find comfort in everything; the soul that complains can find comfort in nothing.

—

Hannah Whitall Smith

Tips for Busy Moms

Help your kids learn to count . . . their blessings! We live in a prosperous society where children may take many of their blessings for granted. Your job, as a responsible parent, is to help your children understand how richly they have been blessed.

— — — — — — — — —

Each child whose heart is filled with inner peace, compassion and acceptance will grow up to become a beacon for peace on Earth. When we feel what others feel, our understanding will be real differenccs will disappear, loving kindness will be here every day, every night, show you care every day, every night, say a little prayer.[27]

Justmommies.com

✳ **Mommy Time** ✳

What are some of the blessings God has showered
upon your family? Do your kids fully
understand the magnitude of these gifts?

_____

_____

_____

_____

_____

_____

_____

_____

_____

_____

_____

_____

_____

_____

Chapter 29

The Wisdom
Not to Judge

Do not judge, and you will not be judged.
Do not condemn, and you will not be condemned.
Forgive, and you will be forgiven.

Luke 6:37 NIV

A funny card said, "I can spot a judgmental person just by looking at them . . ." Okay, Mom, answer honestly: Are you one of those people who finds it easy to judge others? Even if you don't come right out and say anything, do you think it? If so, it's time to make radical changes in the way you view the world and the people who inhabit it.

When considering the shortcomings of others, you must remember this: in matters of judgment, God does not need (or want) your help. Why? Because God is perfectly capable of judging the human heart . . . while you are not.

All of us have all fallen short of God's laws, and none of us, therefore, are qualified to "cast the first stone." Thankfully, God has forgiven us, and we, too, must forgive others. Let us refrain, then, from judging our loved ones, our friends, and our church family. Instead, let us forgive them and love them in the same way that God has forgiven us.

Christians think they are prosecuting attorneys
or judges, when, in reality,
God has called all of us to be witnesses.

—

Warren Wiersbe

Tips for Busy Moms

To the extent you judge others, so, too, will you be judged. So you must, to the best of your ability, refrain from judgmental thoughts and words.

— — — — — — — — —

Healthy habits are the foundation of good time management, and steady morning and evening routines are no exception. Each morning, decide what you're having for dinner (if you haven't already), move the laundry to the next stage, and empty the dishwasher. Every evening, tidy up the house, run the dishwasher, and set out everything you'll need to get the kids out the door such as backpacks and lunch boxes for a streamlined exit in the morning.[28]

GoodHousekeeping.com

✳ **Mommy Time** ✳

Are you sometimes quick to criticize?
If so, what rewards would be yours if you
could learn to be just a little less judgmental?

_____

_____

_____

_____

_____

_____

_____

_____

_____

_____

_____

_____

_____

_____

Chapter 30

Have a Good Laugh!

*There is a time for everything, and everything
on earth has its special season. There is a time to cry
and a time to laugh. There is a time to be
sad and a time to dance.*

Ecclesiastes 3:1,4 NCV

A mother's responsibilities should not be so burdensome that she forgets to laugh. Laughter is medicine for the soul, but sometimes, amid the stresses of the day, we forget to take our medicine. Instead of viewing our world with a mixture of optimism and humor, we allow worries and distractions to rob us of the joy that God intends for our lives.

You are in for a miserable time if you cannot laugh at yourself and your situations. Better still, if you have a friend who "gets" your sense of humor—you are blessed to enjoy a good ol' tears-streaming-down-the-face, no-one-else-would-understand belly laugh! As you go about your daily activities, approach life with a smile on your lips and hope in your heart. Laugh every chance you get—especially with your children. After all, God created laughter for a reason . . .

I want to encourage you in these days
with your family to lighten up and enjoy.
Laugh a little bit; it might just set you free.

—

Dennis Swanberg

Tips for Busy Moms

If you can't see the joy and humor in everyday life . . . you're not paying attention to the right things. Remember the donut-maker's creed: "As you travel through life brother, whatever be your goal, keep your eye upon the donut, and not upon the hole."

— — — — — — — — —

A little humor, a little innovation, a little creativity and, frankly, learning the skill of "letting it go and blowing it off" is a big part of being a happier, more realistic and peaceful working mom.[29]

FocusontheFamily.com

The Busy Mom's Book of Inspiration

✳ **Mommy Time** ✳

Spend a few moments writing down some of the zany things your children have said. ✳

_____

_____

_____

_____

_____

_____

_____

_____

_____

_____

_____

_____

_____

_____

_____

Chapter 31

Getting to Know Him

Be still, and know that I am God.

Psalm 46:10 NKJV

Do you ever wonder if God is really "right here, right now"? Do you wonder if God hears your prayers, if He understands your feelings, or if He really knows your heart? When you have doubts, remember this: God isn't on a coffee break, and He hasn't moved out of town. He's right here, right now, listening to your thoughts and prayers, watching over your every move.

When a dating couple is in a relationship, they want to spend as much time as possible together to get to know one other. Likewise, you'll never know God any better if you never spend time with Him. The Bible teaches that a wonderful way to get to know God is simply to be still and listen to Him.

Some people find quiet moments in their favorite recliner before the kids are up. Others find their haven of rest in the bathroom! Wherever and whenever you can quiet yourself and acknowledge His presence, God can touch your heart and restore your spirit. So why not let Him do it right now? If you really want to know Him better, silence is a wonderful place to start.

The moment you wake up each morning,
all your wishes and hopes for the day rush at you
like wild animals. And the first job each morning
consists in shoving it all back; in listening to that
other voice, taking that other point of view,
letting that other, larger, stronger,
quieter life come flowing in.

—

C. S. Lewis

Tips for Busy Moms

If you'd like to get to know God a little better, talk to Him more often. The more often you speak to Him, the more often He'll speak to you.

— — — — — — — — —

What does intentionally showing your child how to live God's way look like? It looks like tiny steps taken every single day. It requires joyfully showing and telling them some of the same things over and over. It is being transparent with them from day one so they not only understand what the goal is, but they will also desire it themselves. It starts with the faith in your own heart. It starts today, whether your children are tiny or taller than you are.[30]

FocusontheFamily.com

✳ Mommy Time ✳

Write down a few specific things you can do
to help your children know God better.

Chapter 32

God's Timetable

Wait for the Lord; be strong and take heart.
Wait for the Lord.

Psalm 27:14 NIV

If you're in a hurry for good things to happen to you and your family, you're not the only mom on the block who feels that way. But sometimes, you'll simply have to be patient. There's that pesky word again: patience. No matter how many times we hear it, it never sounds any better or any more achievable than the last time we heard it.

God has created a world that unfolds according to His own timetable, not ours . . . thank goodness! We mortals, who have a very limited view of the big picture, would probably make a terrible mess of things. God does not.

Of course, God's plans do not always unfold according to our own wishes, or at the time of our own choosing.

Nonetheless, we should trust the benevolent, all-knowing Father as we wait patiently for Him to reveal Himself. Until God's plans are made clear to us, we must walk in faith and never lose hope, knowing that His plans are always best. Always.

If you want to hear God's voice clearly and you are uncertain, then remain in His presence until He changes that uncertainty. Often, much can happen during this waiting for the Lord. Sometimes, he changes pride into humility, doubt into faith and peace.

—

Corrie ten Boom

Tips for Busy Moms

Trust God's Timing: God has very big plans in store for your life, so trust Him and wait patiently for those plans to unfold. And remember: God's timing is best, so don't allow yourself to become discouraged if things don't work out exactly as you wish. Instead of worrying about your future, entrust it to God. He knows exactly what you need and exactly when you need it.

— — — — — — — — —

These days, there is an app for everything. Take advantage of technology to help save time and your sanity.[31]

Sheknows.com

* Mommy Time *

Make a short list of some things you'd like to accomplish in the years ahead. Are you impatient for these things, or are you willing to trust God's timing?

Chapter 33

When You Have Doubts

If any of you lacks wisdom, you should ask God,
who gives generously to all without finding fault,
and it will be given to you. But when you ask, you must
believe and not doubt, because the one who doubts is like
a wave of the sea, blown and tossed by the wind.

James 1:5–6 NIV

If you're a mom who's never had any doubts about her faith, then you can stop reading this devotion now and skip to the next one. But if you've ever been plagued by doubts about your faith or your God, keep reading.

Even some of the most faithful Christians are, at times, burdened with occasional bouts of discouragement and doubt. But even when we feel distant from God, God is never far removed from us. He is always with us—always willing to replace our doubts with comfort and assurance.

Whenever you're filled with doubts, you might as well tell Him—He knows it anyway. Try to focus on situations when He helped you in the past—times that showed His faithfulness that maybe you have forgotten. Then you may rest assured that, in time, God will calm your fears, answer your prayers, and restore your confidence.

Mark it down. God never turns away
the honest seeker. Go to God with your questions.
You may not find all the answers,
but in finding God,
you know the One who does.

—

Max Lucado

Tips for Busy Moms

When doubts creep in, as they will from time to time, we need not despair. As Sheila Walsh observed, "To wrestle with God does not mean that we have lost faith, but that we are fighting for it."

— — — — — — — — —

Stop comparing yourself and your children to others. Just like you shouldn't compare your children to other children, the same goes for you. Let go of any need you have to compare yourself to other moms.[32]

Justmommies.com

✳ **Mommy Time** ✳

What doubts do you have about your life or
the lives of your family that you need
to turn over to God?

_____

_____

_____

_____

_____

_____

_____

_____

_____

_____

_____

_____

_____

_____

Chapter 34

Time for Fun

So I recommend having fun, because there is nothing better for people to do in this world than to eat, drink, and enjoy life. That way they will experience some happiness along with all the hard work God gives them.

Ecclesiastes 8:15 NLT

Are you a mom who takes time each day to really enjoy life and your family? The Christian life is not a dull gray life of rules with no fun. Whoever thinks that has missed the point: Jesus came to give us life—really big abundant life.

Do you play hide-and-seek with the kids for the hundredth time and build hideouts with a couple of chairs and and a big blanket? Hopefully so. After all, you have been given much to celebrate. And because God has seen fit to give you these gifts, you need to kick back and enjoy them. And if you think you need to go on vacation and spend a lot of money to have fun, children most often remember the simple things—things like running through the backyard with a jar in their hand, trying to capture an elusive firefly, or building a lopsided snowman on a winter's day. You deserve to have fun today, and God wants you to have fun today . . . so, Mom, what on earth are you waiting for?

Whence comes this idea that if what we are doing
is fun, it can't be God's will? The God who made
giraffes, a baby's fingernails, a puppy's tail,
a crooknecked squash, the bobwhite's call,
and a young girl's giggle, has a sense of humor.
Make no mistake about that.

—

Catherine Marshall

Tips for Busy Moms

Since you're a Christian, you have so many things to celebrate today. So make this day, and every day, a cause for celebration, for joy, and for good, healthy fun.

— — — — — — — —

Don't have lots of time for your Family Fun Night? Do the kids still need to be in bed by 8? Keep it short and sweet. You do the planning and keep things moving.

Start out with a fun meal. Move onto a couple of quick rounds of a favorite game. Finish up with a fun dessert.[33]

iMOM.com

✳ **Mommy Time** ✳

What are some fun new things you and your
family can do together in the next 30 days?
And what about bigger adventures you
can plan during the next year?

_____

_____

_____

_____

_____

_____

_____

_____

_____

_____

_____

_____

_____

_____

_____

Chapter 35

Living without Fear

The Lord himself goes before you and will be with you;
he will not leave you nor forsake you.
Do not be afraid; do not be discouraged.

Deuteronomy 31:8 NIV

This world can be a frightening place, where life-changing losses can be so painful and so profound that it seems we will never recover. But, with God's help, and with the help of encouraging family members and friends, we can recover.

Maybe you are in a dark season of life right now, where everyone else appears to be trial-free and seemingly happy. Do not always accept the façade that people present. More people are hurting than they let on. Be honest with God about your feelings, and perhaps share your heart with a close friend.

This valley you may be in won't last forever. Remind yourself of God's promises, even if you don't feel them. "Even if I walk through a very dark valley, I will not be afraid, because you are with me" (Psalm 23:4 HCSB). He is with you. He is for you. And He will carry you.

I have found the perfect antidote for fear.
Whenever it sticks up its ugly face,
I clobber it with prayer.

—

Dale Evans Rogers

Tips for Busy Moms

If you are a disciple of the risen Christ, you have every reason on earth—and in heaven—to live courageously. And that's precisely what you should do.

— — — — — — — — —

Trust God to handle the problems that are simply too big for you to solve. Entrust the future—your future—to God.

— — — — — — — — —

Pray. Only your heavenly father knows everything you're facing in a given day and how it's making you feel. And He cares. Spending a little time each day clearing your heart and mind and talking it out with Him is a sure-fire way to get back on track.[34]

iMOM.com

The Busy Mom's Book of Inspiration

✳ Mommy Time ✳

✳ What are some things that make you fearful?
Have you talked to God about these fears?

_____

_____

_____

_____

_____

_____

_____

_____

_____

_____

_____

_____

_____

_____

_____

Chapter 36

Celebrate!

Rejoice in the Lord always.
I will say it again: Rejoice!
Philippians 4:4 NIV

Did you have a mother or grandmother who owned a beautiful china cabinet filled with pristine china plates and matching cups and saucers? You know, the ones only used for "special occasions"? Maybe they were set out once or twice a year at family get-togethers like Christmas and Thanksgiving. Using them sparingly certainly made them feel special, but any day can be a celebration when we realize the possibilities God gives us each day.

Our responsibility—both as mothers and as believers—is to use this day in the service of God's will and in the service of His people. When we do so, we enrich our own lives and the lives of those whom we love. So, if you have "special occasion" dishes that are just sitting on display, involve your children and tell them today is going to be a celebration! Prepare a tasty meal that they will enjoy—even if it's just an ordinary Monday, it's a cause to celebrate.

Enjoy the little things,
for one day you may look back and
realize they were the big things.

—

Robert Bault

Tips for Busy Moms

If you don't feel like celebrating, start counting your blessings. Before long, you'll realize that you have plenty of reasons to celebrate.

— — — — — — — — —

When you celebrate God's gifts and place God's promises firmly in your mind and your heart, you'll find yourself celebrating life.

— — — — — — — — —

If you want to have fun and enjoy each other, it is helpful to have a catalyst, a rally point, a reason to celebrate. Some families are better than others at celebration moments, but we can all train ourselves to see potential reasons to celebrate.[35]

iMOM.com

The Busy Mom's Book of Inspiration

✳ **Mommy Time** ✳

What are some noteworthy accomplishments that
you and your family haven't yet celebrated?

_____

_____

_____

_____

_____

_____

_____

_____

_____

_____

_____

_____

_____

_____

_____

_____

Chapter 37

Priorities for the Day

He said to them all, "If anyone desires to come after Me,
let him deny himself, and take up his cross daily,
and follow Me. For whoever desires to save his life will
lose it, but whoever loses his life for My sake will save it."

Luke 9:23-24 NKJV

"First things first." These words are easy to speak but hard to put into practice, especially for busy mothers. Why? Because so many people are tugging for Mom's attention—figuratively and literally.

If you're having trouble prioritizing your day, perhaps you've been trying to organize your life according to your own plans, not God's. Maybe you are a "box checker," who finds great satisfaction systematically ticking off all of your tasks for the day. Maybe lists aren't your thing, choosing rather to "wing it" and hope you get everything done.

A better strategy is to take your daily obligations and place them in the hands of the One who created you. Ask God to help you accomplish what needs to be done, and let go of the other things you think have to be done. Then, you can face the day with the assurance that the same God who created our universe out of nothingness will help you place first things first in your own life.

Great relief and satisfaction can come from seeking God's priorities for us in each season, discerning what is "best" in the midst of many noble opportunities, and pouring our most excellent energies into those things.

—

Beth Moore

Tips for Busy Moms

Unless you put first things first, you're bound to finish last. And don't forget that putting first things first means God first and family next.

— — — — — — — — —

When you are missing large quantities of time with your children, you need to be careful that the time you do spend with them is quality-based. Little moments matter. Carve out time and use it wisely. Remember when those moments arrive, to really listen to your kids. Be present with them. Turn off your phone. When you are home, be home and leave work at work—don't let it distract you mentally from being with your family.[36]

Justmommies.com

The Busy Mom's Book of Inspiration

✳ **Mommy Time** ✳

What are your very highest priorities?
Make a short list of them below.

_____

_____

_____

_____

_____

_____

_____

_____

_____

_____

_____

_____

_____

_____

_____

Chapter 38

The Wisdom to Be Generous

You must each decide in your heart how much to give.
And don't give reluctantly or in response to pressure.
"For God loves a person who gives cheerfully."

2 Corinthians 9:7 NLT

A re you a cheerful giver? If you're a mom who's intent upon obeying God's commandments, you must be. When you give, God looks not only at the quality of your gift, but also at the condition of your heart. If you give generously, joyfully, and without complaint, you obey God's Word. But, if you make your gifts grudgingly, or if the motivation for your gift is selfish, you disobey your Creator, even if you have tithed in accordance with biblical principles.

Giving doesn't always mean money; time is a valuable resource that can be given in service to others. One mom may love to cook a meal for another family who just had a baby or is experiencing sickness. Doing so cheerfully is just as important to God as writing a check. Don't devalue what you can give to others. Today, Mom, find ways to be a cheerful and generous giver. The world needs your help, and you need the spiritual rewards that will be yours when you give faithfully. Your children will learn the joy of giving by watching you.

We can't do everything,
but can we do anything more valuable
than invest ourselves in another?

—

Elisabeth Elliot

Tips for Busy Moms

Being kind is a learned behavior. You're the teacher. Class is in session. Your child is in attendance. Actions speak louder than words. And it's one of the most important courses you will ever teach.

— — — — — — — — —

It's never too early to emphasize the importance of giving. From the time that a child is old enough to drop a penny into the offering plate, we, as parents, should stress the obligation that we all have to share the blessings that God has shared with us.

The Busy Mom's Book of Inspiration

✳ **Mommy Time** ✳

Who are some people who really
need your help right now?
Jot down specific things you can do for them.

_____

_____

_____

_____

_____

_____

_____

_____

_____

_____

_____

_____

_____

_____

_____

Chapter 39

Strength for the Day

And He said to me, "My grace is sufficient for you,
for My strength is made perfect in weakness."

2 Corinthians 12:9 NKJV

Some days we just wake up exhausted . . . and the thought of completing an entire day before getting to crawl back in bed at night seems almost impossible. Go to God as you stumble toward the shower (or the coffee pot), and tell Him you feel weak. He delights in supplying His children with strength. God loves you and He will enable you to make it through this day—hour by hour, moment by moment.

When you turn your thoughts and prayers to your heavenly Father, He will give you the energy and the perspective to complete the most important items on your to-do list. And then, once you've done your best, leave the rest up to God. He can handle it . . . and will.

God does not dispense strength and
encouragement like a druggist fills your
prescription. The Lord doesn't promise to give us
something to take so we can handle our weary
moments. He promises us Himself.
That is all. And that is enough.

—

Charles Swindoll

*Those who hope in the LORD will renew
their strength. They will soar on wings like eagles;
they will run and not grow weary,
they will walk and not be faint.*

—

Isaiah 40:31 NIV

Tips for Busy Moms

Exercise is a major stress-buster and mood-lifter, but moms are too busy to hit the gym when the kids are around. If you work outside the home, use your lunch break to fit in a workout or a brisk walk with a colleague. If you're a stay-at-home mom, take your little one out for fresh air in the stroller or baby jogger, or do an exercise video when your tot is napping.[37]

Bettermommies.com

— — — — — — — — —

Try this experiment: for one week, go to bed one hour earlier than you usually do, every night. Don't veg out in front of the TV or the iPad. See how much more energy you have by the beginning of the next week.[38]

webmd.com

✳ **Mommy Time** ✳

Think of times in your life when God came to
the rescue? Write down a few of those times
and thank Him (again) for His strength.

Chapter 40

Controlling Your Temper

My dear brothers and sisters, be quick to listen,
slow to speak, and slow to get angry.
Your anger can never make things right in God's sight.

James 1:19–20 NLT

Motherhood is rewarding, but every mom knows that little frustrating things can build up and cause a big angry explosion. No family is perfect, and even the most loving mother's patience can, on occasion, wear thin.

Your temper is either your master or your servant. Either you control it, or it controls you. And the extent to which you allow anger to rule your life will determine, to a surprising degree, the quality of your relationships with others and your relationship with God.

If you've allowed anger to become a regular visitor at your house, you should pray for wisdom, for patience, and for a heart that is so filled with forgiveness that it contains no room for bitterness. God will help you terminate your tantrums if you ask Him to—and that's a good thing because anger and peace cannot coexist in the same mind. You setting the tone and mood for your home helps your children see how to deal with their frustrations too.

So the next time you're tempted to lose your temper over the minor inconveniences of life, don't. Turn away from anger, hatred, bitterness, and regret. Turn instead to God. He's waiting with open arms . . . patiently.

Go off by yourself. Get down on your knees and just lift up your hands to the Lord and say, "Lord, here is this anger. In the name of Jesus Christ, I surrender it to Your authority. By Your grace, I will not take it back." It's amazing. It's a simple, little act and God hears prayers like that and He loves to answer prayer like that.

—

Elisabeth Elliot

Tips for Busy Moms

Don't Fan the Flames: When your children become angry or upset, you'll tend to become angry and upset, too. Resist that temptation. As the grown-up person in the family, it's up to you to remain calm, even when other, less mature members of the family can't.

— — — — — — — — —

Getting your kids (and yourself) out the door in the morning can be a struggle. Do as much as you can the night before to get prepared. By doing a little extra the night before, you can cut down on the chaos in the morning, when people are tired and more irritable.[39]

Sheknows.com

The Busy Mom's Book of Inspiration

✽ **Mommy Time** ✽

What are some of the everyday frustrations
that always seem to make you angry?
What, if anything, can you do about them?

_____

_____

_____

_____

_____

_____

_____

_____

_____

_____

_____

_____

_____

Chapter 41

Beyond Guilt

*So now, those who are in Christ Jesus are not
judged guilty. Through Christ Jesus the law of
the Spirit that brings life made you free from
the law that brings sin and death.*

Romans 8:1–2 NCV

All of us have made mistakes. Sometimes our failures result from our own shortsightedness. On other occasions, we are swept up in events that are beyond our abilities to control. Under either set of circumstances, we may experience intense feelings of guilt. But God has an answer for the guilt that we feel. That answer, of course, is His forgiveness. If He's forgiven it, then why are we walking around with it chained to our leg? We rob ourselves of peace and joy today when we remain captive to a past sin or mistake—as if our penance will pay for the offense. Jesus paid it all.

When we ask our Heavenly Father for His forgiveness, He forgives us completely and without reservation. Then, we must do the difficult work of forgiving ourselves in the same way that God has forgiven us: thoroughly and unconditionally.

If you're feeling guilty, then it's time for a special kind of housecleaning—a housecleaning of your mind and your heart . . . beginning NOW!

Don't be bound by your guilt or
your fears any longer, but realize that
sin's penalty has already been paid by
Christ completely and fully.

Billy Graham

Tips for Busy Moms

If you've asked for God's forgiveness, He has given it. But have you forgiven yourself? If not, the best moment to do so is this one.

— — — — — — — — —

That same forgiveness you give to your child when she does wrong is available to you, too, from a gracious and loving Heavenly Father. When you've confessed and apologized, trust Him enough to just accept the forgiveness He offers and use it as inspiration to live a life that's pleasing to Him going forward. Guilt is not your friend, and it doesn't make you a better mom. Learning and growing does![40]

iMOM.com

✳ **Mommy Time** ✳

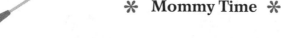

Think about times when God forgave you,
but you couldn't seem to forgive yourself.
Jot down your thoughts about God's willingness
to forgive and your willingness to accept it.

_____

_____

_____

_____

_____

_____

_____

_____

_____

_____

_____

_____

_____

_____

Chapter 42

Finding Hope

Now may the God of hope fill you with all joy
and peace as you trust in him, so that you may overflow
with hope by the power of the Holy Spirit.

Romans 15:13 NIV

Sometimes we just don't feel very hopeful, whether because of discouraging circumstances or just a bleak outlook. Hope is more than just an emotion, however; it is a discipline, a determination to believe in God's ability to love and care for you.

When a suffering woman sought healing by merely touching the hem of His cloak, Jesus replied, "Daughter, be of good comfort; thy faith hath made thee whole" (Matthew 9:22 KJV). The message to believers is clear: if we are to be made whole by God, we must live by faith.

If you find yourself falling into the spiritual traps of worry and discouragement—or just feeling "blah"—seek the healing touch of Jesus and the encouraging words of fellow Christians. (This is where surrounding yourself with positive people can really make a difference!) Your hope is in God—He's never going to leave you, and He always keeps His promises.

You can look forward with hope,
because one day there will be no more separation,
no more scars, and no more suffering in My
Father's House. It's the home of your dreams!

—

Anne Graham Lotz

Tips for Busy Moms

If you're experiencing hard times, you'll be wise to start spending more time with God. And if you do your part, God will do His part. So never be afraid to hope—or to ask—for a miracle.

— — — — — — — — —

If you find yourself in a tough situation this week, shift your focus from what is going wrong to how you can excel by relying on the gifts God has given you. A prayer that helped me last week was asking God for a heart of service and joy in doing so, so that no matter how the day went, I could walk in humility and keep my eyes peeled for opportunities to bless others.[41]

FocusontheFamily.com

✳ **Mommy Time** ✳

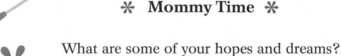

What are some of your hopes and dreams?
Do you trust God's timetable for
accomplishing those things?

_____

_____

_____

_____

_____

_____

_____

_____

_____

_____

_____

_____

_____

_____

_____

Chapter 43

What's Your Talent?

Do not neglect the gift that is in you.

1 Timothy 4:14 NKJV

Each and every woman possesses special gifts, talents, and opportunities—you are no exception. God created you with special skills to use for His glory—and to make you smile and feel happy too!

When trying to figure out what your talent is, please do not compare yourself with other moms. Everyone is different. One mother may be great at planning and organizing events, creating committees, and making elaborate Excel spreadsheets; while another may be one of those crafty moms who can whip up a beautiful topiary centerpiece out of pinecones, a foam ball, and an old wine bottle! Today, Mom, accept this challenge: value the talent that God has given you. Nourish it, make it grow, and share it with the world. And while you're at it, you can help your children discover what their God-given talents and gifts are. Thank God that He made each one to be unique and special.

Not everyone possesses boundless energy
or a conspicuous talent. We are not equally
blessed with great intellect or physical beauty
or emotional strength. But we have all been
given the same ability to be faithful.

—

Gigi Graham Tchividjian

Tips for Busy Moms

Of course you want to help your child discover his or her hidden—or not so hidden—talents. A good place to start is by helping your child discover the topics and activities that are the most fun. Today's child's play may become tomorrow's passionate pursuit.

— — — — — — — — —

When you engage in an activity that you really enjoy, time seems to fly. The moment is meaningful; you feel fully alive. Taking time to share what you're good at, develop what interests you, or engage in what brings you joy adds meaning to life.[42]

Live.FamilyEducation.com

✳ **Mommy Time** ✳

Think about your talents and opportunities.
What are some ways you can use God's gifts to
achieve your dreams and serve His children?

_____

_____

_____

_____

_____

_____

_____

_____

_____

_____

_____

_____

_____

_____

Chapter 44

Making Peace
with the Past

Forget the former things; do not dwell on the past.
See, I am doing a new thing! Now it springs up;
do you not perceive it? I am making a way in
the wilderness and streams in the wasteland.

Isaiah 43:18–19 NIV

Are there some things in your past that haunt you—that you just can't let go of? If you are mired in the quicksand of regret, it's time to plan your escape. How can you do so? By accepting what has been and moving on to trust God for what will be.

It is human nature to be slow to forget yesterday's disappointments. Don't forget that Satan loves to remind us of our past mistakes—he keeps us weak when we feel defeated. But if you sincerely seek to focus your hopes and energies on the future, then you must find ways to accept the past, no matter how difficult it may be to do so.

So, Mom, here's a powerful piece of advice: If you have not yet made peace with the past, today is the day to declare an end to all regret. Wishing you could go back in time and change things does no good. It's futile. Move forward from this moment . . . turn your thoughts to the glorious future that God has in store for you.

Yesterday is just experience but tomorrow
is glistening with purpose—and today is
the channel leading from one to the other.

—

Barbara Johnson

Tips for Busy Moms

The past is past, so don't invest all your energy there. If you're focused on the past, change your focus. If you're living in the past, move on.

— — — — — — — — —

Post it. Hang a family wall calendar to keep track of everything from PTA meetings to doctor visits to movie dates with your husband. Post an ongoing grocery list on the fridge. Buy an erasable white board and hang it in the kitchen to post lists and reminders.[43]

Parents.com

✳ **Mommy Time** ✳

What are some things that have been tough for you to accept? How often have you asked God to help you accept the past and move on?

_____

_____

_____

_____

_____

_____

_____

_____

_____

_____

_____

_____

_____

Chapter 45

God's Gift to You: Your Children

Start children off on the way they should go,
and even when they are old they will not turn from it.

Proverbs 22:6 NIV

Everyone knows that children are a gift from God. As a mother, you have been entrusted by God with a priceless treasure: your child. Every child is different and unique, and will require different parenting skills. There is no cookie-cutter formula when raising multiple children—even in the same house.

The most important thing you can do for your child is to pray. And pray in specific terms. Pray for small but meaningful things, like their day at school—that they will do their best on their spelling test or the science presentation on the solar system. Pray for big, futuristic things, like God's direction—that He will guide them toward a college where He wants them to be, or your child's future spouse that they haven't even met yet.

Thoughtful mothers (like you) understand the critical importance of raising their children with love, with discipline, and with God. By making God a focus in the home, loving mothers offer a priceless legacy to their children—a legacy of hope, a legacy of love, a legacy of wisdom.

Today, pray for your children . . . pray specifically for their concerns, no matter how small.

Children are not casual guests in our home.
They have been loaned to us temporarily
for the purpose of loving them and
instilling a foundation of values
on which their future lives will be built.

—

James Dobson

Tips for Busy Moms

Taking care of children is demanding, time-consuming, energy-depleting . . . and profoundly rewarding. Simply put, your child is a marvelous gift from God. And, your opportunity to be a parent is yet another gift, for which you should give thanks.

— — — — — — — — —

Try this: look at your child and smile. Keep smiling. If they ask you what you're smiling about, say, "It just makes me happy to be your mom."[44]

iMOM.com

The Busy Mom's Book of Inspiration

✳ **Mommy Time** ✳

Make a list of creative things you can do to
show your kids that you love them.

_____

_____

_____

_____

_____

_____

_____

_____

_____

_____

_____

_____

_____

_____

_____

Chapter 46

Beyond Failure

Even though good people may be bothered
by trouble seven times, they are never defeated.

Proverbs 24:16 NCV

The occasional disappointments and failures of life are inevitable. Such setbacks are simply the price that we must occasionally pay for our willingness to take risks as we follow our dreams. But even when we encounter bitter disappointments, we must never lose faith.

As a mom, you may have experienced failure; but you are not a failure. You are far from perfect; and neither are your children. What's important is learning from your mistakes. Zig Ziglar wisely said, "If you learn from defeat, you haven't really lost."

Hebrews 10:36 advises, "Patient endurance is what you need now, so you will continue to do God's will. Then you will receive all that he has promised" (NLT). These words remind us that when we persevere, we will eventually receive the rewards which God has promised us. In the meantime, while we are waiting for God's plans to unfold, we can be comforted in the knowledge that our Creator can overcome any obstacle, even if we cannot.

One of the ways God refills us after failure is through the blessing of Christian fellowship. Just experiencing the joy of simple activities shared with other children of God can have a healing effect on us.

Anne Graham Lotz

Tips for Busy Moms

Almost every major failure in life—whether it's related to love, health, money, or anything else—is simply the result of many little failures along the way that were never attended to. Little failures add up if you let them . . . so don't let them.

— — — — — — — — —

Learn to say no. One reason why busy moms are so busy is because they have difficulties saying no. You don't have to say no to everything, but if you are feeling stressed and overworked, it is time for you to put yourself first and start saying no.[45]

JustMommies.com

The Busy Mom's Book of Inspiration

✳ **Mommy Time** ✳

What are some of your biggest disappointments
in life? What did you learn from
those disappointments?

_____

_____

_____

_____

_____

_____

_____

_____

_____

_____

_____

_____

_____

_____

Chapter 47

Listening to God

My sheep hear My voice, and I know them,
and they follow Me. And I give them eternal life,
and they shall never perish; neither shall anyone
snatch them out of My hand."

John 10:27–28 NKJV

Sometimes God speaks loudly and clearly. More often, He speaks in a quiet voice—and if you are wise, you will be listening carefully when He does. To do so, you must carve out quiet moments each day to study His Word and sense His direction. This is not a time to read e-mails on your phone or check in "real quick" on Facebook.

Quietness is a discipline no different than other disciplines, like exercising or watching what you eat. Can you quiet yourself long enough to listen to your conscience? Are you attuned to the subtle guidance of your intuition? These are just fancy words for the Holy Spirit inside of us.

Wouldn't it be great if God sent us blatant personal messages written in the sky or on a billboard?! However, that's not the way He operates. He communicates in subtler ways.

When you are parenting babies and small children, quiet times are extremely difficult. But don't give up, assuming you need an hour and a half of quiet time for the Lord to speak. Maybe all you have to offer are ten minutes—then offer those precious ten minutes. If you're a mom who sincerely desires to hear His voice, then listen in the silent corners of your willing heart.

When we come to Jesus stripped of pretensions,
with a needy spirit, ready to listen,
He meets us at the point of need.

—

Catherine Marshall

Tips for Busy Moms

Having trouble hearing God? If so, slow yourself down, tune out the distractions, and listen carefully. God has important things to say; your task is to be still and listen. Your children are depending upon it.

— — — — — — — — —

Start and end your day with peace. Try to set aside even just a few minutes of quiet time in your own little corner of your home at the beginning and end of each day.[46]

Live.FamilyEducation.com

The Busy Mom's Book of Inspiration

✳ **Mommy Time** ✳

✳ What messages do you think God might be
trying to get through to you? ✳

_____

_____

_____

_____

_____

_____

_____

_____

_____

_____

_____

_____

_____

_____

_____

Chapter 48

Find Your Happy Place

But happy are those . . . whose hope
is in the Lord their God.

Psalm 146:5 NLT

Okay, Mom, it's been a typical day. You've cared for your family, worked your fingers to the bone, rushed from Point A to Point Z, and taken barely a moment for yourself. But have you taken time to smile? To laugh? If not, it's time to slow down, take a deep breath, and recount your blessings!

Not taking your situation too seriously is key to enjoying your day more. Kids, in and of themselves, can provide a plethora of funny material! One good idea to remembering the humorous things that happen to you throughout the day is to keep a Smile Notebook. Jot down the cute way your kids pronounce words, like "ska-betti" or "thinger." Write down that you got your four small kids packed and ready for a day at the zoo thirty miles away only to hear your seven-year-old say, "Mommy, I forgot to put on my shoes . . ."

Relax and learn the art of being happy—let go of a lot of things that really don't matter anyway. When you do, you'll discover that when you smile at your family and at God, He smiles back.

When we bring sunshine into the lives of others,
we're warmed by it ourselves.
When we spill a little happiness, it splashes on us.

—

Barbara Johnson

Tips for Busy Moms

Happiness is a positive interpretation of the world and its events. Happiness requires that you train yourself to see the good in everything, no matter what happens.

— — — — — — — — —

Find the humor in life. If you tend to be fascinated by bad news or sad stories, don't always share the grim and unfortunate things of life with your kids. Look for joy and laugh when you find it.[47]

iMOM.com

The Busy Mom's Book of Inspiration

✳ **Mommy Time** ✳

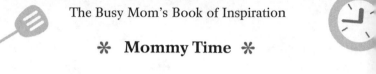

What are some of life's little luxuries that
make you happy?

_____

_____

_____

_____

_____

_____

_____

_____

_____

_____

_____

_____

_____

_____

_____

Chapter 49

Detours on the Journey

*But blessed are those who trust in the LORD
and have made the LORD their hope and confidence.
They are like trees planted along a riverbank, with roots
that reach deep into the water. Such trees are not
bothered by the heat or worried by long months
of drought. Their leaves stay green, and
they never stop producing fruit.*

Jeremiah 17:7–8 NLT

When life unfolds according to our wishes, or when we experience unexpected good fortune, we find it easy to praise God's plan. That's when we greet change with open arms. The job promotion came through; the house finally sold. But sometimes the changes that we must endure are painful. When we struggle on a path that suddenly takes a detour from where we thought we were going, we may ask ourselves, "Why is this happening? And why now?" The answer, of course, is that God knows, but He isn't telling . . . yet.

Have you endured a difficult transition that has left your head spinning or your heart broken? Maybe you've experienced a unexpected move to a new community where you know no one. Maybe it's just a feeling deep down that this isn't where you saw yourself at this stage in your life. If so, you have a clear choice to make: either you can cry and complain, or you can trust God that He knows best and get busy fixing what's broken in your heart. So, Mom, with no further delay, let the fretting cease, and let the fixing begin.

When faced with adversity the Christian woman
comforts herself with the knowledge
that all of life's events are in the hands of God.

—

Vonette Bright

Tips for Busy Moms

If you're facing big-time adversity don't hit the panic button and don't keep everything bottled up inside. Instead of going underground, talk things over with your husband, with your friends, with your pastor, and if necessary, with a trained counselor. When it comes to navigating the stormy seas of life, second, third, fourth, or even fifth opinions can sometimes be helpful.

— — — — — — — — —

Sometimes we just need to talk it out, to vent, or to worry out loud for a second. A wise friend can offer valuable perspective on your situation, and can tell you when you're making a mountain out of a molehill.[48]

iMOM.com

The Busy Mom's Book of Inspiration

✳ **Mommy Time** ✳

How do you deal with change? What are some
specific things you can do to make big-time
changes easier for you and your family?

_____

_____

_____

_____

_____

_____

_____

_____

_____

_____

_____

_____

_____

_____

_____

Chapter 50

Encouraging Words

I want you woven into a tapestry of love,
in touch with everything there is to know of God.
Then you will have minds confident and at rest,
focused on Christ, God's great mystery.

Colossians 2:2 MSG

Every member of your family needs a regular supply of encouraging words and pats on the back. And you need the rewards that God gives to enthusiastic moms who are a continual source of encouragement to their families.

In his letter to the Ephesians, Paul writes, "Let everything you say be good and helpful, so that your words will be an encouragement to those who hear them" (4:29 NLT). This passage reminds us that, as Christians, we are instructed to choose our words carefully so as to build others up through honest encouragement. How can we build others up? By celebrating their victories and their accomplishments. Children are thirsty for praise—some more than others. Notice good behavior, pay attention to the effort they give to something, even if it didn't turn out quite right, and always have room on the refrigerator for another smiley-face drawing. As the old saying goes, "When someone does something good, applaud—you'll make two people happy."

Today, look for the good in others—starting with your family. And then, celebrate the good that you find. When you do, you'll be a powerful force of encouragement in your corner of the world—the corner that God has given just for you.

Don't forget that a single sentence,
spoken at the right moment, can change
somebody's whole perspective on life.
A little encouragement can go a long, long way.

Marie T. Freeman

Tips for Busy Moms

Encouragement is an essential ingredient in healthy parent-child communications. Make sure that you encourage your child by communicating your love, your admiration, and your devotion—and make certain that you do so many times each day.

— — — — — — — — —

Encouraging children's efforts spurs on their learning. This is the good news! When a child grows up in a home with loving parents and an atmosphere of encouragement, it fosters mental growth.[49]

FocusontheFamily.com

The Busy Mom's Book of Inspiration

✳ Mommy Time ✳

Who are some people who might really need your encouragement today? What specific things could you do to encourage them?

_____

_____

_____

_____

_____

_____

_____

_____

_____

_____

_____

_____

_____

_____

Chapter 51

Walking with the Wise

Listen to advice and accept correction,
and in the end you will be wise.

Proverbs 19:20 NCV

Okay Mom, here's a simple yet effective way to strengthen your faith: Choose role models whose faith in God is strong.

When you emulate godly women, you become a more godly woman yourself. You must surround yourself with people who, by their words and their presence, make you a better woman (and mother). And, to the best of your ability, you must avoid those people who encourage you to think foolish thoughts or do foolish things.

Today, as a gift to yourself and your family, select, from your friends and family members, a mentor whose judgment you trust. Then listen carefully to your mentor's advice and be willing to accept that advice, even if accepting it requires effort, or pain, or both. Consider your mentor to be God's gift to you. Thank God for that gift, and use it wisely . . . and often.

The effective mentor strives to help
a man or woman discover what they can be
in Christ and then holds them accountable
to become that person.

—

Howard Hendricks

Tips for Busy Moms

Think about the mentors who have had a positive impact on your own life. Then think about ways you can be a positive influence on your children.

— — — — — — — — —

Think of a mom you admire? Ask yourself what quality of hers can you live out today.[50]

iMOM.com

— — — — — — — — —

A good mentor is a person who you naturally enjoy being with, who has more experience than you have, who would be happy to help you win in life, to help you grow in sensitive areas most other friends simply "put up with" on a day to day basis.[51]

FocusontheFamily.com

✳ **Mommy Time** ✳

Who are the friends and mentors whose
judgment you trust most?
How often do you turn to them for advice?

_____

_____

_____

_____

_____

_____

_____

_____

_____

_____

_____

_____

_____

_____

_____

Chapter 52

God Rested—
So Should You

Remember the Sabbath day, to keep it holy.

Exodus 20:8 NKJV

When God gave Moses the Ten Commandments, it became perfectly clear that our heavenly Father intends for us to make the Sabbath a holy day—a day for worship, for contemplation, for fellowship, and for rest. Yet we live in a seven-day-a-week world, a world that all too often treats Sunday as a regular workday.

How does your family observe the Lord's day? Perhaps by the time you get the kids ready, yourself ready, and the Bibles and shoes gathered, you may not even be thinking about the holiness of the day. When church is over, do you treat Sunday like any other day of the week? If so, it's time to think long and hard about your family's schedule and your family's priorities.

Whenever we ignore God's commandments, we pay a price. So if you've been treating Sunday as just another day, it's time to break that habit. When Sunday rolls around, don't try to fill every spare moment. God did not intend for it to be a "catch-up" day for all things left undone from the busy week. Take time to truly rest . . . Father's orders!

God did not just cease from his labor;
he stopped and enjoyed what he had made.
What does this mean for us? We need to stop
to enjoy God, to enjoy his creation, to enjoy
the fruits of our labor. The whole point of
Sabbath is joy in what God has done.

—

Tim Keller

Tips for Busy Moms

As a parent, you decide how your family will spend Sundays. The Sabbath is unlike any other day. Your job is to observe the Sabbath, not ignore it.

— — — — — — — — —   .

I need not do it all every Sunday. My husband and I can switch off Sundays, giving each other a turn at having a relaxing, meditative Sunday. The kids can be expected to clean up after themselves (or just not make any messes for ONE day every week) and to help with the younger kids.[52]

Icecreamdiary.blogspot.com

The Busy Mom's Book of Inspiration

✳ Mommy Time ✳

What's the right amount of sleep for you and your kids? And what specific things can you do to be sure that all of you get enough rest.

_____

_____

_____

_____

_____

_____

_____

_____

_____

_____

_____

_____

_____

_____

_____

216

Chapter 53

Your Real Treasures

I will bless them and the places surrounding my hill.
I will send down showers in season;
there will be showers of blessings.

Ezekiel 34:26 NIV

Sometimes we need to be reminded of the treasure box we have—a box filled with jewels like life, family, freedom, friends, talents, and possessions, for starters. God has given you blessings that are, in truth, simply too numerous to count. But, your greatest blessing—a priceless treasure that is yours for the asking—is God's gift of salvation through Christ Jesus.

The old hymn reminds us to "Count your blessings, name them one by one. And it will surprise you what the Lord hath done." It's hard to worry about stuff when you're counting your blessings. And the gifts you receive from God are multiplied when you share them with others.

Today, give thanks to God for your blessings and demonstrate your gratitude by sharing those blessings with your family, with your friends, and with the world.

Do we not continually pass by blessings innumerable without notice, and instead fix our eyes on what we feel to be our trials and our losses, and think and talk about these until our whole horizon is filled with them, and we almost begin to think we have no blessings at all?

—

Hannah Whitall Smith

Tips for Busy Moms

Carve out time to thank God for His blessings. Take time out of every day (not just on Sundays) to praise God and thank Him for His gifts.

— — — — — — — — —

God wants to bless you abundantly and eternally. When you trust God completely and obey Him faithfully, you will be blessed.

— — — — — — — — —

Take time to thank God for the blessings that He has given to you and your family.[53]

FocusontheFamily.com

The Busy Mom's Book of Inspiration

✳ Mommy Time ✳

Some of God's blessings are numerous
and so common that we may be tempted
to take them for granted.
What blessings have you overlooked lately?

_____

_____

_____

_____

_____

_____

_____

_____

_____

_____

_____

_____

_____

_____

Chapter 54

His Strength Is Perfect

And He said to me, "My grace is sufficient for you,
for My strength is made perfect in weakness."

2 Corinthians 12:9 NKJV

Of this you can be certain: God is sufficient to meet your needs. Period.

The demands of motherhood may seem overwhelming at times. You may feel like you are just trying to "get through the day" until bedtime. That's not living; that's existing. Remember that God always uses weak people to display His strength. God will hold your hand and walk with you and your family if you let Him. So even if your circumstances are difficult, trust the Father.

The psalmist writes, "Weeping may endure for a night, but joy comes in the morning" (Psalm 30:5 NKJV). But when we are suffering, the morning may seem very far away. It is not. God promises that He is "near to those who have a broken heart" (Psalm 34:18 NKJV). When we are troubled, we must turn to Him.

If you are discouraged, don't just exist. Choose His strength working through you so that you can truly live today. The loving heart of God is sufficient to meet any challenge . . . including yours.

The last and greatest lesson that the soul has to
learn is the fact that God, and God alone,
is enough for all its needs. This is the lesson that
all His dealings with us are meant to teach;
and this is the crowning discovery of our whole
Christian life. God is enough!

—

Hannah Whitall Smith

Tips for Busy Moms

Whatever your weaknesses, God is stronger. And His strength will help you measure up to His tasks.

— — — — — — — — —

Today, think about ways that you can tap into God's strength: try prayer, worship, and praise, for starters.

— — — — — — — — —

Stuff = Time. The more stuff you have in your home, the more cleaning, dusting, and organizing you need to do. If your house is bursting at the seams, it might be time for a yard sale or big donation to Goodwill or the Salvation Army.[54]

Live.FamilyEducation.com

✻ Mommy Time ✻

How do you respond to God when you feel weak?
What are some specific things you can do to
remind yourself of His power and His love?

_____

_____

_____

_____

_____

_____

_____

_____

_____

_____

_____

_____

_____

_____

The Direction of Your Thoughts

Fix your thoughts on what is true and honorable and right. Think about things that are pure and lovely and admirable. Think about things that are excellent and worthy of praise.

Philippians 4:8 NLT

Thoughts are intensely powerful things. Our thoughts have the power to lift us up or drag us down; they have the power to energize us or deplete us, to inspire us to greater accomplishments or to make those accomplishments impossible.

How will you direct your thoughts today? Will you obey the words of Philippians 4:8 by dwelling upon those things that are honorable, true, and worthy of praise? Or will you allow your thoughts to be hijacked by the negativity that seems to dominate our troubled world?

Are you fearful, angry, bored, or worried? Are you so preoccupied with the concerns of this day that you fail to thank God for the simple pleasure of your child's smile, or the bigger gift of His promise of eternity? Are you bitter or pessimistic? If so, God wants to have a little talk with you.

God intends that you experience joy and abundance, but He will not force His joy upon you—you must claim it for yourself. It's up to you to celebrate the life that God has given you by focusing your minds upon things that are "lovely and admirable." Your attitude affects your family, especially your children. They have sensors that pick up on your negative moods. So form the habit of spending more time thinking about your blessings and less time fretting about your hardships.

The mind is like a clock that is constantly
running down. It has to be wound up
daily with good thoughts.

—

Fulton J. Sheen

Tips for Busy Moms

By speaking words of thanksgiving and praise, you honor the Father and you protect your heart against the twin evils of apathy and ingratitude.

— — — — — — — — —

Many moms are disappointed when their children don't naturally show great kindness towards others or a good attitude, but these are actually skills that are learned and developed over time. So begin now by teaching your children how to share a good attitude with others and to treat others with kindness.[55]

iMOM.com

✳ **Mommy Time** ✳

How does your attitude affect the attitude of your
kids, and vice versa? What specific things can
you do to improve everybody's attitude?

_____

_____

_____

_____

_____

_____

_____

_____

_____

_____

_____

_____

_____

_____

_____

_____

Chapter 56

Dangerous Media Messages

Set your minds on things that are above,
not on earthly things.

Colossians 3:2 NIV

The media is working around the clock in an attempt to rearrange your family's priorities in ways that may not always be in your best interests. All too often, the media teaches your family that physical appearance is all-important, that material possessions should be acquired at any cost, and that the world operates independently of God's laws. But guess what? Those messages are untrue.

So here's an important question, Mom: Will you control what appears on your TV screen, or will your family be controlled by it? If you're willing to take complete control over the images that appear inside the four walls of your home, you'll be doing your clan a king-sized favor.

So today, with no further delay, take control of your family's remote, mouse, and smart phone. You'll be glad you did, and so, in a few years, will they.

While it's one thing to talk about media discernment, it's another thing to spell out expectations and boundaries in writing. A written media covenant placed in a prominent location serves as a constant reminder of its importance.

—

James Dobson

Tips for Busy Moms

Monitor the images that your children view on television and on the Internet. You, as a responsible parent, must decide which messages and which images are appropriate for your child. The responsibility is yours and yours alone, not that of television executives or web page designers.

— — — — — — — — — —

Parents today have a lot of tasks that demand their time—cleaning, cooking, banking, laundry, chauffeuring—the list goes on and on. Yet there's another critical role crying for attention in many homes: family media guardian.[56]

FocusontheFamily.com

The Busy Mom's Book of Inspiration

✳ Mommy Time ✳

Specifically, what media choices are good for
your family, and what media choices
are potentially harmful?
Make a list and talk to your kids about it.

_____

_____

_____

_____

_____

_____

_____

_____

_____

_____

_____

_____

_____

_____

Chapter 57

Overcoming Worry

Let not your heart be troubled;
you believe in God, believe also in Me.

John 14:1 NKJV

If you are like most mothers, it is simply a fact of life: from time to time, you worry. You worry about your kids, about your health or your family's health, about finances, about safety, and about countless other challenges of life, some great and some small. Where is the best place to take your worries? Take them to God. Carrying them yourself is an exercise in futility, as you probably have already figured out. Take your troubles to God, and your fears, and your sorrows.

Barbara Johnson correctly observed, "Worry is the senseless process of cluttering up tomorrow's opportunities with leftover problems from today." So if you'd like to make the most out of this day (and every one hereafter), turn your worries over to a Power greater than yourself . . . and spend your valuable time and energy solving the problems you can fix—while trusting God to do the rest.

Today is mine. Tomorrow is none of my business.
If I peer anxiously into the fog of the future,
I will strain my spiritual eyes so that
I will not see clearly what is required of me now.

Elisabeth Elliot

Tips for Busy Moms

Categorize Your Worries: Carefully divide your areas of concern into two categories: those things you can control and those you cannot control. Once you've done so, spend your time working to resolve the things you can control, and entrust everything else to God.

— — — — — — — — —

Being a mother can be great fun. But every now and then you run across a mom who makes your head spin. The lady doesn't know when to quit. Often, these women are insecure in their own situations and that's why they give you such grief.[57]

Life.FamilyEducation.com

✳ **Mommy Time** ✳

Make a list of things you're worried about but
cannot control. Then, ask God to help you
turn those worries over to Him.

_____

_____

_____

_____

_____

_____

_____

_____

_____

_____

_____

_____

_____

_____

_____

Chapter 58

Your Journey with God

*For God is working in you, giving you the desire
and the power to do what pleases him.*

Philippians 2:13 NLT

Life is best lived on purpose, not by accident. The sooner we discover what God intends for us to do with our lives, the better. But God's purposes aren't always clear to us. Sometimes, the responsibilities of caring for our loved ones leave us precious little time to discern God's will for ourselves. At other times, we may struggle mightily against God in a vain effort to find success and happiness through our own means, not His.

Whenever we struggle against God's plans, we suffer. When we resist God's calling, our efforts bear little fruit. Our best strategy, therefore, is to seek God's wisdom and follow Him wherever He chooses to lead. When we do so, we are blessed.

When you arrive at one of life's crossroads—wondering which way do I go?—that is precisely the moment when you should turn your thoughts and prayers toward God. When you do, He will make Himself known to you in a time and manner of His choosing. He has a definite plan for your life!

One thing is certain, even if everything else is blurry: God purposed for you to be a mother. And you can rejoice that you are fulfilling that plan right now . . . today.

Great relief and satisfaction can come from seeking God's priorities for us in each season, discerning what is "best" in the midst of many noble opportunities, and pouring our most excellent energies into those things.

—

Beth Moore

Tips for Busy Moms

God has a wonderful plan for your life. And the time to start looking for that plan—and living it—is now. (*You make known to me the path of life; you will fill me with joy in your presence, with eternal pleasures at your right hand.* Psalm 16:11 NIV)

— — — — — — — — —

God's plans are unfolding day by day. And if you keep your eyes and your heart open, He'll reveal His plans. God has big things in store for you, but He may have quite a few lessons to teach you before you are fully prepared to do His will and fulfill His purposes.

✳ **Mommy Time** ✳

What are some of the greatest joys you
derive from being a mom?

_____

_____

_____

_____

_____

_____

_____

_____

_____

_____

_____

_____

_____

_____

_____

_____

Chapter 59

Worthy to Be Loved

*For God so loved the world that he gave his one
and only Son, that whoever believes in him
shall not perish but have eternal life.*

John 3:16 NIV

As a mother, you know the profound love that you hold
in your heart for your own children. Well, multiply that
by about a thousand, then maybe you can get a glimpse of
God's infinite love for you.

You are worthy to be loved! You don't have to maintain a standard in order to receive that love—it's a gift made
possible through His Son Jesus Christ. It's His righteousness that you now have. You can't lose your worth, either. It's
unconditional.

There are many things, however, that can make us feel
worthless: bad choices in our past, if we've been cheated on

or abused, if we don't earn a big paycheck, or if someone has ever told us that we were worthless. These are lies that Satan uses to keep us from the love and joy we have in Christ. And they are very effective, aren't they?

When you embrace God's love, you are forever changed—you feel differently about yourself, your neighbors, your family, and your world. Today, when you look in the mirror, see yourself in a new way: a woman who is made in the image of God—precious and valuable, worthy to be loved.

Accepting God's love as a gift instead of trying to earn it had somehow seemed presumptuous and arrogant to me, when, in fact, my pride was tricking me into thinking that I could merit His love and forgiveness with my own strength.

—

Lisa Whelchel

Tips for Busy Moms

Remember: God's love for you is too big to understand with your brain . . . but it's not too big to feel with your heart.

— — — — — — — — —

Remember that God's love doesn't simply flow to your children . . . it flows to you, too. And because God loves you, you can be certain that you, like your child, are wonderfully made and amazingly blessed.

— — — — — — — — —

Remember how much you've been loved. God has shown His love for each of us in innumerable ways. Is it so much to ask us just to pay that forward to others?[58]

iMOM.com

The Busy Mom's Book of Inspiration

✳ **Mommy Time** ✳

What does the promise of John 3:16 mean to you? Jot down your ideas and talk to your kids about it.

_____

_____

_____

_____

_____

_____

_____

_____

_____

_____

_____

_____

_____

_____

Chapter 60

Thanks, Mom

Her children rise up and call her blessed.

Proverbs 31:28 NKJV

Everyone needs to hear a heartfelt thank-you from time to time. It gives us affirmation that what we are doing really matters. It also gives us strength to keep on giving, even when we don't feel like it. We conclude with a message of thanks to you, a busy mom who doesn't have it all together, but you trust the One who does:

Dear Mom,

Thanks for the love, the care, the hard work, the discipline, the wisdom, the support, and the faith. Thanks for being a concerned parent and a worthy example. Thanks for giving life and for teaching it. Thanks for being patient, even when you were tired, or frustrated—or both. Thanks for changing diapers, wiping away tears, and reading the bedtime books. And thanks for being a godly woman, one worthy of our admiration and our love.

You deserve a smile today, Mom, but you deserve so much more. You deserve our family's undying gratitude. And, you deserve God's love, His grace, and His peace. May you enjoy God's blessings always, and may you never, ever forget how much we love you.

Signed,
Your Loving Family

The mother is and must be, whether she knows it
or not, the greatest, strongest,
and most lasting teacher her children have.

—

Hannah Whitall Smith

Tips for Busy Moms

Make sure that your family's spiritual foundation is built upon "the rock": Mom, you are, without question, your child's most important teacher. Make sure that your family's curriculum includes lots of lessons from the Bible.

— — — — — — — — —

When you place your faith in God, life becomes a grand adventure energized by the power of God. Good luck, Mom, on the next stage of your own grand adventure!

✳ **Mommy Time** ✳

Make a quick list of things you appreciate about your kids. Then, thank each of them individually for the joy and love you feel in your heart.

_____

_____

_____

_____

_____

_____

_____

_____

_____

_____

_____

_____

_____

_____

Let the Word of Christ—the Message—have the run of the house. Give it plenty of room in your lives. Instruct and direct one another using good common sense. And sing, sing your hearts out to God! Let every detail in your lives—words, actions, whatever—be done in the name of the Master, Jesus, thanking God the Father every step of the way.

—

Colossians 3:16-17 MSG

Helpful Websites and Blogs
Quoted in This Book

247Moms.com

FamilyEducation.com

FocusontheFamily.com

GoodHousekeeping.com

iMOM.com

JustMommies.com

Live.FamilyEducation.com

Parenting.com

SheKnows.com

TheOnlineMom.com

WebMD.com

To Find More Mommy Bloggers,
Check Out These Sites

MommyBloggerDirectory.com

CircleOfMoms.com

TopMommyBlogs.com

MomBloggersClub.com

Endnotes

1-"How to Love Your Kids Without Losing Your Mind," © 2011 iMOM, all rights reserved, http://www.imom.com/mom-life/encouragement/how-to-love-your-kids-without-losing-your-mind/ (Family First, All Pro Dad, iMOM, and Family Minute with Mark Merrill are registered trademarks).

2-Gina Costa, "15 Time-Management Tips," American Baby, http://www.parents.com/parenting/moms/healthy-mom/time-management-tips/.

3-Sarah Mahoney, "Busy Moms—Slow Down and Feel the Joy," http://www.parents.com/parenting/moms/healthy-mom/busy-moms-slow-down-and-feel-the-joy/?page=3.

4-Lorie Marrero, "11 Scheduling Secrets of Busy Moms," http://www.goodhousekeeping.com/family/scheduling-secrets-busy-moms-children-activities#slide-8.

5-Stephanie Gates, "Moms Who Change the World, Part Four," http://www.mops.org/moms-who-change-the-world-part-four.

6-Lorie Marrero, "11 Scheduling Secrets of Busy Moms," http://www.goodhousekeeping.com/family/scheduling-secrets-busy-moms-children-activities#slide-4.

7-"How to Change Your Negative Thinking," © 2011 iMOM, all rights reserved, http://www.imom.com/parenting/toddlers/relationships/family/how-to-change-your-negative-thinking/ (Family First, All Pro Dad, iMOM, and Family Minute with Mark Merrill are registered trademarks).

8-"Proclaim Your Love of Life," http://life.familyeducation.com/organization/stress/56282.html.

9-Walt Larimore, MD, "The Attributes of Great Parents," taken with permission from Walt Larimore, MD, with Stephen and Amanda Sorenson, God's Design for the Highly Healthy Child (Highly Healthy Series), http://www.imom.com/mom-life/encouragement/the-attributes-of-great-parents/.

10-Steph Fink, "In the Space Between Perfect and Me," http://247moms.com/2013/10/in-the-space-between-perfect-and-me/.

11-Gina Costa, "15 Time-Management Tips," American Baby, http://www.parents.com/parenting/moms/healthy-mom/time-management-tips/.

12-Michelle LaRowe, "Making Mornings Manageable," http://www.focusonthefamily.com/parenting/parenting_roles/working-moms-organizing-your-day/making-mornings-manageable.aspx.

13-Erin Dower, "12 Real Time-Savers for Busy Moms," http://life.familyeducation.com/time-management/family-routines/73090.html.

14-Julie Ferwerda, "Should we go?" vs. "Why shouldn't we go?", http://247moms.com/2013/04/should-we-go-vs-why-shouldnt-we-go/.

15-"Stress: Reducing Your Stress and Anger," © 2011 iMOM, all rights reserved, http://www.imom.com/mom-life/wellness/stress-reducing-your-stress-and-anger/ (Family First, All Pro Dad, iMOM, and Family Minute with Mark Merrill are registered trademarks).

16-"How to Get Out of the House on Time with Kids," http://www.aupairjobs.com, in http://247moms.com/2013/07/how-to-get-out-of-the-house-on-time-with-kids/.

17-Tracey Eyster, Guest iSpecialist, "Your Attitude is a Choice," http://www.imom. com/mom-life/encouragement/your-attitude-is-a-choice/.

18-"9 Ways to Be Worthy of Imitation," © 2013 iMOM, all rights reserved, http://www.imom.com/mom-life/encouragement/9-ways-to-be-worthy-of-imitation/ (Family First, All Pro Dad, iMOM, and Family Minute with Mark Merrill are registered trademarks).

19-Gina Shaw, "9 Energy Tips for Moms," http://www.webmd.com/parenting/family-health-12/energy-tips-moms.

20-Ziona Hochbaum, "10 Stress-busting Tips for Busy Moms," http://www.parenting.com/article/10-stress-busting-tips-for-busy-moms.

21-Michelle LaRowe, "Working Moms: Organizing Your Day," http://www.focusonthefamily.com/parenting/parenting_roles/working-moms-organizing-your-day.aspx.

22-Sue Clashower, "Monday Motivation: God Has a Special Plan for Someone Like You," http://busymomsconnect.com/monday-motivation-discover-gods-plan/.

23-"Time: 8 Ways to Simplify Your Life," © 2011 iMOM, all rights reserved, http://www.imom.com/mom-life/mom-management/time-8-ways-to-simplify-your-life/ (Family First, All Pro Dad, iMOM, and Family Minute with Mark Merrill are registered trademarks).

24-Kori Ellis, "10 Sanity and time-saving tips for moms on the go," http://www.shcknows.com/parenting/articles/967891/10-sanity-and-time-saving-tips-for-moms-on-the-go.

25-"30 Day Mom Challenge," http://www.imom.com/pages/30-day-mom-challenge/.

26-Gina Costa, "15 Time-Management Tips," American Baby, http://www.parents.com/parenting/moms/healthy-mom/time-management-tips/.

27-Patti Teel, "Return to the Spirit of Mothers Day," http://www.justmommies.com/articles/spirit-of-mothers-day.shtml.

28-Lorie Marrero, "11 Scheduling Secrets of Busy Moms," http://www.goodhousekeeping.com/family/scheduling-secrets-busy-moms-children-activities#slide-10.

29-Michelle LaRowe, "Working Moms: Organizing Your Day," http://www.focusonthefamily.com/parenting/parenting_roles/working-moms-organizing-your-day.aspx.

30-Mark Holmen, "Passing on Faith Requires Intentionality," adapted from Faith Begins at Home and Faith Begins @ Home Dad (Regal, 2007, 2010), all rights reserved, used by permission, http://www.focusonthefamily.com/parenting/spiritual_growth_for_kids/faith at home/passing-on-faith-requires-intentionality.aspx.

31-Kori Ellis, "Time Savers for Busy Moms," http://www.sheknows.com/parenting/articles/967891/10-sanity-and-time-saving-tips-for-moms-on-the-go.

32-Lori Radun, "5 Ways to Zap 'Mommy Guilt,'" http://www.justmommies.com/family-life/just-for-moms/5-ways-to-zap-mommy-guilt.

33-"Short and Sweet Family Fun Night," © 2011 iMOM, all rights reserved, http://www.imom.com/mom-life/family-fun/short-and-sweet-family-fun-night/ (Family First, All Pro Dad, iMOM, and Family Minute with Mark Merrill are registered trademarks).

34-"15 Things to Do When You Feel Overwhelmed," © 2011 iMOM, all rights reserved, http://www.imom.com/mom-life/encouragement/15-things-to-do-when-you-feel-overwhelmed/ (Family First, All Pro Dad, iMOM, and Family Minute with Mark Merrill are registered trademarks).

35-Fred Hartley, "5 Building Blocks to 'I-Like-You' Families," taken with permission from Hartley's Parenting at Its Best! How to Raise Children with a Passion for Life!, http://www.imom.com/parenting/tikes/relationships/family/5-building-blocks-to-i-like-you-families/.

36-"The Working Mom Juggle: How to Make Time for Your Kids Without Dropping the Ball," http://www.justmommies.com/family-life/just-for-moms/the-working-mom-juggle-how-to-make-time-for-your-kids-without-dropping-the?slide=2.

37-"10 Stress-Busting Tips from Moms Like You," http://www.bettermommies.com/10-Stress-Busting-Tips-from-Moms-Like-You_ad-id!81.ks.

38-Gina Shaw, "9 Energy Tips for Moms," http://www.webmd.com/parenting/family-health-12/energy-tips-moms?page=2.

39-Kori Ellis, "Time Savers for Busy Moms," http://www.sheknows.com/parenting/articles/967891/10-sanity-and-time-saving-tips-for-moms-on-the-go.

40-"4 Ways to Show Yourself Grace," © 2012 iMOM, all rights reserved, http://www.imom.com/mom-life/encouragement/4-ways-to-show-yourself-grace/ (Family First, All Pro Dad, iMOM, and Family Minute with Mark Merrill are registered trademarks).

41-Amy Seed, "When Things Go Wrong," July 17, 2013, https://community.focusonthefamily.com/b/boundless/archive/2013/07/17/when-things-go-wrong.aspx.

42-"Feed a Passion," http://life.familyeducation.com/organization/stress/56267.html.

43-Gina Costa, "15 Time-Management Tips," American Baby, http://www.parents.com/parenting/moms/healthy-mom/time-management-tips/.

44-"6 Ways to Be a Joyful Mom," © 2012 iMOM, all rights reserved, http://www.imom.com/mom-life/encouragement/6-ways-to-be-a-joyful-mom/ (Family First, All Pro Dad, iMOM, and Family Minute with Mark Merrill are registered trademarks).

45-"10 Organization Tips for Busy Mom," http://www.justmommies.com/family-life/home-organization/10-organization-tips-for-busy-mom.

46-Erin Dower, "10 Stress-Busting Tips from Moms Like You," http://life.familyeducation.com/slideshow/womens-health/69774.html.

47-"6 Ways to Be a Joyful Mom," © 2012 iMOM, all rights reserved, http://www.imom.com/mom-life/encouragement/6-ways-to-be-a-joyful-mom/ (Family First, All Pro Dad, iMOM, and Family Minute with Mark Merrill are registered trademarks).

48-"15 Things to Do When You Feel Overwhelmed," © 2011 iMOM, all rights reserved, http://www.imom.com/mom-life/encouragement/15-things-to-do-when-you-feel-overwhelmed/ (Family First, All Pro Dad, iMOM, and Family Minute with Mark Merrill are registered trademarks).

49-Cheri Fuller, "Boost Learning Power," adapted from Handbook on Choosing Your Child's Education, a Focus on the Family book (Tyndale House Publishers, 2007), all rights reserved, international copyright secured, used by permission, http://www.focusonthefamily.com/parenting/schooling/equip_kids_for_learning/boost_learning_power.aspx.

50-"30 Day Mom Challenge," http://www.imom.com/pages/30-day-mom-challenge/.

51-Bobb Biehl, "What to Look for in a Mentor," from Biehl's Mentoring: How to Find a Mentor and How to Become One (Aylen Publishing, 2005), all rights reserved, international copyright secured, used by permission, http://www.focusonthefamily.com/marriage/strengthening_your_marriage/mentoring_101/what_to_look_for_in_a_mentor.aspx.

52-Ice Cream, "Can Moms Keep the Sabbath Day Holy?", http://icecreamdiary.blogspot.com/2008/04/can-moms-keep-sabbath-day-holy.html.

53-Mark Holmen, "Pray with Your Children," adapted from Faith Begins at Home (Regal, 2007), all rights reserved, used by permission, http://www.focusonthefamily.com/parenting/spiritual_growth_for_kids/faith-at-home/pray-with-your-children.aspx.

54-"12 Real Time-Savers for Busy Moms," http://life.familyeducation.com/time-management/family-routines/73090.html?page=10.

55-"Attitudes: Sharing a Good Attitude," Random Acts of Kindness Foundation, © 2007 iMOM, all rights reserved, http://www.imom.com/parenting/teens/relationships/social/attitudes-sharing-a-good-attitude/.

56-Rhonda Handlon, "The Family Media Guardian," http://www.focusonthefamily.com/parenting/protecting_your_family/the-family-media-guardian.aspx.

57-"Dealing with Other Mothers," http://life.familyeducation.com/mothers/parenting/57108.html.

58-"4 Ways to Love the Difficult People in Your Life," © 2012 iMOM, all rights reserved, http://www.imom.com/mom-life/encouragement/4-ways-to-love-the-difficult-people-in-your-life/ (Family First, All Pro Dad, iMOM, and Family Minute with Mark Merrill are registered trademarks).

*The good people who live
honest lives will be
a blessing to their children.*

—

Proverbs 20:7 NCV